Re-Inventing Chenille

Fresh Sewing Techniques and P

Nannette Holmberg

Re-Inventing Chenille

Fresh Sewing Techniques and Projects

Nannette Holmberg

KRAUSE PUBLICATIONS
CINCINNATI, OHIO

mycraftivity.com
connect. create. explore.

Other fine Krause Publications titles are available from your local bookstore, craft supply store, online retailer or visit our website at www.fwpublications.com.

13 12 11 10 09   5 4 3 2 1

Distributed in Canada by Fraser Direct
100 Armstrong Avenue
Georgetown, ON, Canada L7G 5S4
Tel: (905) 877-4411

Distributed in the U.K. and Europe by David & Charles
Brunel House, Newton Abbot, Devon, TQ12 4PU, England
Tel: (+44) 1626 323200, Fax: (+44) 1626 323319
Email: postmaster@davidandcharles.co.uk

Distributed in Australia by Capricorn Link
P.O. Box 704, S. Windsor NSW, 2756 Australia
Tel: (02) 4577-3555

Library of Congress Cataloging in Publication Data
Holmberg, Nannette, 1948-
  Re-inventing chenille : fresh sewing techniques and
  projects / Nannette Holmberg.-- 1st ed.
      p. cm.
  Includes index.
ISBN 978-0-89689-729-8 (pbk. : alk. paper)
1. Sewing. 2. Textile crafts. 3. Chenille. I. Title.
  TT705.H665 2009
  646.2--dc22   2008050620

Edited by Nancy Breen
Designed by Rachael Smith
Production Coordinated by Matt Wagner
Photography by Richard Deliantoni and Tim Grondin

About the Author

Nannette Holmberg studied design at the Fashion Institute of Technology in New York. The originator of Faux Chenille®, she created designs for The McCall Pattern Company before starting her own line of patterns. Her previous books are *New Directions in Chenille* (Martingale & Company, 2000) and *Variations in Chenille* (Martingale & Company, 1997). Nannette's wearable and quilt designs have been shown in the United States, Europe and Japan. Her Chenille-It™ Blooming Bias™ products are sold in shops and online. Nannette lives in Salt Lake City, Utah, with her husband, David.

Metric Conversion Chart

To convert	to	multiply by
Inches	Centimeters	2.54
Centimeters	Inches	0.4
Feet	Centimeters	30.5
Centimeters	Feet	0.03
Yards	Meters	0.9
Meters	Yards	1.1

Acknowledgments

Writing a book is a wonderful experience and, typically, a long journey. It is only with the enthusiasm of your publisher and the assistance of a professional, efficient editor that you are able to pull everything together and attempt to meet deadlines. With heartfelt thanks I acknowledge the help of my editor, Nancy Breen. Working through photo shoots, countless e-mails and the transfer of samples from one end of the country to the other, she was not only helpful but cheerful and even flexible.

I have been fortunate to have friends and companies that have supported my work and been generous with their products. Thanks to them, I have been able to explore the possibilities and experiment with the latest and greatest in the sewing world. My goal is always to find new ways to use basic products in combination with the techniques I have been developing over the years. My thanks to Sulky of America, VSM, Kandi Corp, Things Japanese and Thimbleberries for making my projects the best they could be. I always promise my students that next year I will bring something fresh to (hopefully) inspire them to try something new, to make them think, "What if?" After all, that is the very way every new idea and project begins.

Dedication

This book is dedicted to three very important people:

To my husband David for his unending support, help and encouragement; for endless trips for supplies and filling in with the business when I was too busy to help; for doing the work of two when necessary. I give him full credit for the final completion of this book.

To my daughter Erin, who always encourages me through the toughest and longest days. Her talent and knowledge of photography have helped me more than she will ever know. Her cheerful voice from across the country makes everything possible.

To my mother, affectionately known as "Great Granny," who started me at the tender age of three years by putting a needle and thread in my hand. She made sure I always had what I needed to pursue my dreams and continues to tell me she is proud of what I have been able to accomplish. I stand on her shoulders.

Contents

Chapter One
Chenille: Then and Now

Chapter Two
Transforming Ready-to-Wear

Chapter Three
Recapturing Vintage Style

Chapter Four
Working with Unexpected Materials

Chapter Five
Chenille Texture at Home

Introduction

Adding texture to textile surfaces has been a form of fashion for centuries. Renowned quilting author Virginia Avery has written that slashed fabric was used for clothing in Europe, particularly Germany, as far back as the sixteenth century. Often clothing was slashed to form designs such as flower petals. Leather jackets had slashed sleeves and heavily slashed backs. Today's designers such as Zandra Rhodes and Tim Harding continue to expand fabric slashing techniques to create wearable art.

In the 1800s, machines were invented that pulled thread tufts through woven fabric to create a soft raised design. The fabric commonly became known as *chenille*, very popular in the early twentieth century for bedspreads and in the 1940s and 1950s for bathrobes. The word *chenille* actually originated in France and means *caterpillar*.

Over the years, home sewers and crafters have explored myriad techniques to replicate the soft textures produced on commercial machines. Everything from sweatshirts to silk was stitched, slashed, brushed and washed in an attempt to raise textile surfaces.

Adventures in Texture

In the 1980s, wearable art designer Tim Harding began layering colorful silks and developed a signature look by stitching, slashing and manipulating the cut layers. The result was a wash of changing colors and a rough tactile texture.

I first experimented with texturizing fabrics in the early 1990s. I was fascinated with Harding's designs, but I wanted to find my own style. I began to work with less expensive fabrics, adding couture finishing and my own twist on nontraditional construction and fiber combinations.

I was hooked when I made my first layered jacket with seven layers of rayon stitched on the bias, slashed and washed in the washing machine. When the jacket came out of the dryer, I had a *wow* moment that began a new series of *what if* speculations that continue to this day.

I assumed that Harding left his edges raw and unfinished because of the washing process for the completed jacket. My background in fashion design and bridal and evening couture led me to explore what would happen to these layered jackets if I added fine couture finishing and detail work. What kind of results would I get when these creations were thrown into the washing machine?

Since I didn't want to spend a great deal of money on a project with possibly disastrous results, I experimented with inexpensive rayons from the clearance table. To my surprise, my layered and slashed jacket finished with detailed bias binding and couture detailing went through the washing/drying process beautifully—and the rest is history.

Expanding the Options

I became a designer for McCall's pattern company and introduced the home sewer to a new way to create chenille-like texture. That first experimental jacket became the cover of my first book.

Creating texture with fabric became my obsession, going far beyond the multiple fabric layers that started it all so many years ago. I have combined everything from fine woolens, silks and rayons to the least expensive muslins and other cottons. I've combined all of these fibers with great success and a wide range of resulting textures and weights. I have used this layering technique to make jackets, vests, accessories, quilts and more.

I've continued to experiment, exploring new techniques. Eventually I discovered the excitement of working with continuous bias, breaking the rules of traditional chenille with a new look in texture that is simple, fast and has fabulous results. The projects in the pages that follow will open a new world of possibilities for you as well.

Tools of the (Chenille) Trade

A Few Simple Tools Make a Big Difference
Keep a fringe frame (*left*), a lint roller (*middle*) and a bent wire brush (*right*) at hand when working on the chenille projects in this book.

There are a few basic tools that will make working with the continuous bias easy and your sewing time shorter.

Thread

Always use good quality thread. Bargain basket threads are often weak and sometimes old. If you stitch bias with weak thread, it could break during the washing process or when you're wearing a garment. If a stitch breaks, the fibers and threads it held in place will be lost. It's very disappointing to pull a chenille project from the dryer to find holes and empty spots when there should be a soft chenille texture.

Brushes

You may want to add texture to a garment or home décor project that you don't want to wash. There are also times when you want to add texture to a project that is not machine washable, such as a silk or fine wool. A small bent wire brush is perfect for pulling up the fibers and separating them. The brushing technique gives a soft fringed effect that is

slightly different from the washed fluffy look. The brush is also nice when you want just the edges of the bias frayed for a raw-edged fashion effect.

Lint Roller

You won't lose any threads in the washing process as long as you use the correct stitch length and good quality thread. Some fabrics will, however, lose a little lint or leave it on the edges of the chenille after it is dried.

I like to keep a lint roller handy to run over the finished chenille just to pick up any loosened threads or lint that may remain after going through the drying process. A few minutes with a lint roller will give your texture a nice clean finished look.

Fringe Frame

Continuous bias can be prepared to use like yarn for some dramatic effects. One of my favorite tools for working with prepared bias is what used to be called a fringe, or hairpin lace, frame. These frames are still available in needlework and craft stores or online, and you may even find vintage ones in your grandmother's sewing room or on eBay. There's also a version available called the Loop-dee-Doodle™.

The fringe frame is a U-shaped frame available in a variety of widths and lengths. I like to work with a frame is that is 3" (8cm) wide and 12" to 14" (30cm to 36cm) long. This provides options for finished widths of textured trims as well as fringe.

The prepared bias is wrapped by itself or with yarn around the frame and stitched on the sewing machine to hold the loops together. The stitching holds the bias loops together until you are ready to stitch the fringe to a garment or accessory project as embellishment. You can also run another strip of bias along the prestitched line to reenforce the loops and wash them for a great scarf. (See pages 39–40 for instructions on using the frame and making a looped scarf.)

Additional Tools

There are a few other basic tools you'll find listed in the *Materials List* for each project. These include:

- **Marking tools** such as dressmaker's chalk, fabric marking pencil and wash-away fabric pen.
- **Rotary cutter and cutting mat** for cutting bias strips or fabric for individual projects.
- **Spray-on fabric adhesive or water-soluble fabric glue stick** if you wish to affix fabric pieces without pins.
- **Heat-set applicator** for working with heat-set embellishments like crystals and studs.

There are other materials and tools unique to each project listed in the *Materials List*. Be sure to read each list thoroughly before starting that project.

Of course, you'll be working with your sewing machine, iron and ironing board, scissors and other basic tools you depend on in any type of sewing project.

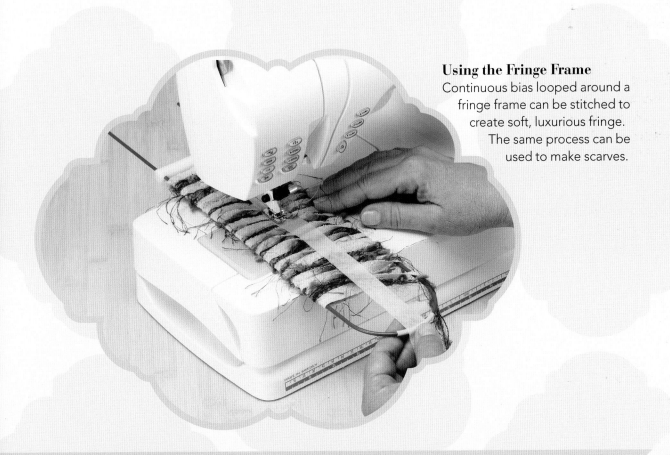

Using the Fringe Frame
Continuous bias looped around a fringe frame can be stitched to create soft, luxurious fringe. The same process can be used to make scarves.

Chapter One

Chenille: Then and Now

To understand the process of working with continuous bias for the chenille projects in this book, it's helpful to review what I now call *traditional chenille*. Examining the stitch-and-slash technique that involves multiple layers of fabric will help you see how my *re-invented chenille* technique works—and why it's so much faster and easier than traditional chenille.

We'll then move on to examining the *re-invented* aspect of chenille: working with continuous bias. From cutting bias strips and stitching precut bias from a roll to working with specialty sewing machine feet and hand-dyeing bias, you'll learn all you need to know to add spectacular texture to your own garments and home decorating projects.

Traditional Chenille: An Overview

I first called my layered jackets *faux chenille* in the early 1990s because the soft, luxurious texture of the rayons I used reminded me of the chenille bedspreads of my grandmother's day. It wasn't long before the sewing industry used my trademarked name of Faux Chenille® when referring to garments made with the stitch-and-slash technique that created this new soft texture. It's also known as traditional chenille.

Using Natural Fibers

There are two keys to success with this technique. First, the cut fabric layers for traditional chenille must be 100 percent natural fibers.

The smallest percentage of synthetic in the weave keeps the cut edges from exploding and blooming, while a touch of polyester in the mix of the top cut layer in the chenille stack will actually prevent the underneath layers from creating this blooming effect. The result will be a chenille stack that is flat and disappointing.

Stitching on the True Bias

The second key to success: The rows of stitching across the chenille stack must be on the true bias of the fabric (i.e., on a 45° angle to the straight of the grain, the vertical and horizontal directions of the threads as they were woven on the loom).

Pulling woven fabric along these vertical and horizontal grain lines results in very little give. However, pulling the fabric on the true bias allows it to stretch.

By stitching on the true bias, you catch the weft and warp yarns of the fabric at the same time. I prefer to sew channels of stitching ½" (13mm) apart for most of my traditional chenille projects. A narrower channel produces a shorter pile of texture, while a wider channel of ⅝" (16mm) or more gives a fuller, deeper texture that reveals more of the base layer.

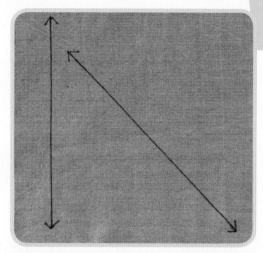

Straight of Grain Versus True Bias

The straight line on the left indicates the straight of grain of the fabric (which runs horizontally as well as vertically). The 45° line (i.e., the diagonal line) shows the true bias of the fabric.

Bringing Out the Texture

Once they're stitched, the chenille layers are cut (slashed) between the rows of stitching, leaving the base layer intact.

After the fabrics are layered, stitched and cut, the garment is constructed; then it is washed on a regular cycle in an agitating machine. Finally, the garment is placed in a dryer until completely dry.

One of the biggest misconceptions about the chenille process is that the chenille texture is created as a result of multiple layers of fabric. It is generally accepted that you must have at least three layers of fabric that are cut in a chenille stack to create the texture we now call "chenille."

Actually, it's not the number of layers, the width of the stitched channels or even the washing process that is critical. Most important are the fabrics themselves.

A Little Sample of Traditional Chenille

Exploring Fabrics

Every piece of fabric has its own characteristics. I've found that fabric of 100 percent natural fibers does not guarantee a desirable chenille texture. That's why fabrics must be tested before they're used for a traditional chenille project.

Many natural fiber fabrics will be a disappointment when tested. Some cottons bloom and others don't. Rayons and silks must also be tested for their "chenille-ability." I've been texturizing fabrics for twenty years and I would not begin without testing a new fabric.

Testing fabrics is a simple and exciting exploration. It's fascinating to see what the final result will be.

Try It for Yourself

If you'd like to learn about the traditional chenille technique (and try a little fabric experimentation of your own), make some sample swatches using four layers of fabric. You can use the same fabric for all four layers or four different pieces, even mixing fibers if you wish.

Stacking

Cut one 5" (13cm) square for the base. Cut three 4" (10cm) squares for the layers that will be slashed (i.e., the chenille layers). If you use the same fabric for all four layers, you need only make one sample. However, if you're using three different fabrics in your chenille layers, experiment! Make three different test swatches, with the top three fabrics layered in a different order for each swatch.

Stack the three 4" squares and center them on top of the 5" square base. With a fabric marking pencil, draw a line from corner to corner (this is your 45° bias line). You may wish to continue to draw lines that are ½" (13mm) apart on either side of the diagonal line or use the edge of your presser foot to gauge ½" (13mm) rows.

Different Combinations, Different Results
Layering the top three fabrics in different order for each test swatch produces a variety of results.

Results with Silk
Handwoven 100% silk is a good candidate for adding texture and interesting colorations to a project.

Luxurious Texture, Interesting Colorations
Compare test results for 100% rayon (brown strip) and 100% loosely woven silk (blue/white strip).

Three Colors Layered Three Ways
Layering three colors in a different order can give you completely different results.

Stitching

Stitch on the marked line through all the fabric layers using a 2.0 stitch length. Continue to stitch rows that are ½" (13mm) apart on either side of the first row of stitching. Continue until the square is filled with ½" diagonal rows or channels of stitching.

Slashing

Through this process you have basically quilted your stack of fabrics together. Because you have a base layer that is larger than the top three layers, it will be easy to slip a pair of blunt-nosed scissors between the rows of stitching and cut (or slash) the three top layers down the middle between the stitched lines.

Test Results

Now the fun begins. Because you're working with a small sample, you'll get the best results by completely wetting the quilted square. Wring out the excess moisture and rub the sample vigorously between your hands to bring up the cut edges. Immediately you'll see if your fabrics worked satisfactorily.

Place the sample swatches with a few towels in the dryer on a medium heat setting. Dry completely. What comes next is my favorite part—you never know what your results will be until this moment.

Producing Different Effects

If you're working with three different fabrics or colors, likely you'll have three totally different sample swatches. A good fabric result will be full and soft with no sign of the original fabrics. If the fabric characteristics are not what they should be (the characteristics are the yarns, the weave and the weight), you may end up with a flat sample with just the top layer showing and the fabric still looking much the same as it did before it was washed. Or the final result may be something between full and flat. This is where you as the designer must decide if this is what you were hoping for or if you should test other fabric combinations.

If a fabric is a good candidate for the chenille process, it will bloom with just one cut layer instead of two or three. A single layer of the right silk, for example, will give a much fuller and softer texture than four or five layers of cotton or rayon. Test different combinations of fabrics and also different numbers of layers.

Re-Inventing the Chenille Technique

After more than fifteen years of creating texture with multiple layers of fabric, I was in the middle of a "research and development" session in my studio when I first had the idea to break away from my usual techniques.

I had found that the best way to finish the edges on my Faux Chenille® jackets was by using a ⅜" to ½" (10mm to 13mm) finished bias binding. This gave a clean finished edge to the jackets without adding bulk.

Binding an edge with a soft, stretchy fabric like rayon took time and extra care for a professional result. Because I was in a time crunch, I decided to explore other possibilities for finishing the raw, cut outer edges of my jackets. I cut some ⅝" (16mm) bias strips from the scraps of one of my jacket's chenille layers and serged the raw edges of the jacket to keep them from fraying. I stitched my cut bias strips to the wrong side of the jacket edges, then stitched a layer of bias to the outside edges. My unfinished edges were now enclosed within bias strips.

I held my breath as I placed the finished jacket in the washer and then the dryer. When I pulled out the dry jacket, I couldn't believe my eyes. The jacket now had a soft textured edge that blended perfectly with the layered cut edges of chenille. Imagine what I could do with these newly discovered simple strips of bias!

This testing process led me to the possibility of working with continuous bias instead of the laborious traditional chenille technique with its multiple layers of fabric. After lots more cutting and testing, I realized I wanted to spend more time playing and less time cutting, so I turned to precut continuous bias on a roll.

Rolls of precut continuous bias in a wide range of colors are available in some shops and online. Because of their time-saving qualities, I use a ⅜" (10mm) or ⅝" (16mm) rolled continuous bias for most of the projects in this book.

NOTE: The following metric equivalents are used routinely throughout this book: ⅜" equals 10mm; ⅝" equals 16mm.

Rolls of Bias
Rolls of precut continuous bias are available commercially in a range of colors. They are easy to overdye as well.

Making Your Own Continuous Bias

Of course, you also have the option of cutting and testing fabrics to make your own continuous bias for all of this book's projects. Take time to test the fabrics you want to use to avoid unhappy surprises later. Testing fabrics for use as continuous bias is much the same as testing fabrics for traditional chenille.

Work with fabric woven from natural fibers. For your test base, use a fabric scrap that's similar to the base you plan to use for your project. Follow the instructions on this page for cutting bias strips—use this technique for cutting test strips as well.

Stitch test bias strips to the base fabric by sewing down the center of the strips with a shortened stitch length of 1.5–2.0. Always use a shorter stitch length when working with loose woven fabrics.

Stitch three rows of test strips to the base fabric: one with a single layer of bias strips, one with a double layer and one with a triple layer. This will help you gauge the fullness you'll get with different numbers of layers. Wash and dry the test swatches in the same manner as the traditional chenille swatches.

The projects in this book have been designed using 100 percent cotton continuous bias that will bloom with a single layer; double layers of bias are also used for various techniques. As you do your own research and development with bias fabrics, remember that creating texture is an exploration with no limits and a world of possibilities. Feel free to play with fabrics in your stash and never be afraid to push the limits!

Cutting Strips of Continuous Bias

1. Using a rotary cutter and a cutting mat, position the fabric and line up the selvage edge with the 45° angle on the ruler. Make the first cut.

2. Line up the cut edge of the fabric with the ⅝" line on the ruler. Cut a strip, realign the edge of the fabric with the ⅝" line, and cut again. Continue until the desired number of strips are cut.

demonstration
Making a Test Swatch

1 Lay down strips of bias in the desired design. *NOTE: Designs may be straight or curved. Pinning is optional*

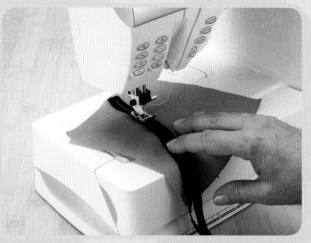

3 Stitch the layered bias into place along the design line using a 2.0 stitch length.

2 Continue to sew strips into place along each line until all design lines are covered.

4 Wet the test swatch thoroughly and wring out the excess water. Rub the swatch between your hands to loosen the bias and cause it to bloom.

Stitching Continuous Bias

Stitching is critical when using continuous bias. Be sure to use a good quality thread. This is not the time to use bargain basket thread that may not be strong and could break when washed. Any thread breakage will result in lost chenille and will leave empty spots in your design.

Stitch length is another critical thing to watch. If you're losing fibers when the sample is washed or dried, try shortening the stitch length on loosely woven bias to ensure that all the fibers are securely caught in the stitching. Doing test swatches with various weights, weaves and fibers will provide a wide range of results.

Repairing Chenille

Empty spots in a chenille design can be repaired by stitching a new cut piece of bias in the space using a shortened stitch length. Brush the new bias section carefully and spritz with water. Place the mended project in the dryer just long enough to dry and fluff the repaired area.

Strips Can Be Overlapped

Whether you're using strips of bias you've cut yourself or bias from a roll, remember that it's not necessary to sew all the individual strips together. When you're sewing the bias to the project fabric, simply add a new strip, overlapping the strip ends, and continue.

Prestitched Bias

You can use continuous bias like yarn for embellishing and for making fringe. The only preparation needed is to run a row of stitching down the center of the tape. All that holds the fibers together is this single row of stitching, so it's critical to use a shortened stitch length when prestitching either ⅜" or ⅝" bias. A 1.0 stitch length ensures that all the crossed threads in the bias are caught and secured. Use the best quality thread for prestitching so none of the threads break in the washing or brushing process.

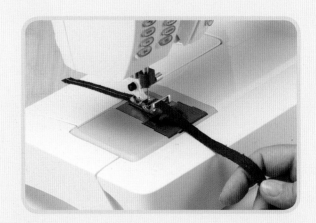

Finishing Edges with Chenille

Finishing edges with chenille is easy and eliminates the bulk of turned seams, facings and hems. Using bias to finish edges is also a great alternative to a bound edge and is much easier and faster to do. The best width for finishing the edges of garments, accessories and home decorator projects is ⅝" bias.

Be sure to zigzag stitch or serge any raw or unfinished edges before applying the bias. Over time, through use or in the washing process, unfinished edges will fray out and lose their threads.

1 Zigzag stitch along the raw edges of the project to stabilize the edge and reduce fraying.

2 On the wrong side of the fabric, stitch bias along all edges with the bias extending about ⅛" (3mm) over the zigzag-stitched edge.

3 When you come to a corner, stitch the bias to the edge. Cut the end of the bias ⅛" (3mm) beyond the corner. Turn and position the bias with the end aligned with the edge you just stitched. Again, the edge of the bias you're beginning to sew should extend about ⅛" (3mm) beyond the zigzag-stitched edge of the project.

Easy Corners

It's not necessary to sew bias around a corner to achieve a finished look. When the project is washed and dried, the bias will bloom, creating a texture that will conceal where the bias stops and starts at the corners.

4 Turn the fabric over and stitch the bias along the edges on the right side. Align the edge of the bias with the bias stitched to the wrong side of the fabric. Turn the corners as described in Step 3.

5 When done, you can either wash and dry the piece, or brush the bias to bring out the texture.

Using Specialty Feet

It's always nice to find a new application for any specialty feet you may have for your sewing machine. When working with continuous bias, it also helps to be able to feed or guide things through the foot. The cording foot for many machines has an opening that's helpful when layering yarn on the bias for added detail.

The Ruffler Foot

The ruffler foot is often neglected, but I like to use it when I have a design that has circular or curved edges. Pleated bias makes an interesting trim for clothing or for home décor projects, and it's easy to shape for swirls or for tight rosettes and circular designs.

Most ruffler feet have a setting for the number of stitches the machine will take before it makes a pleat. I like to set the foot to 6 and set the sewing machine to a 2.0 stitch length for best results.

Feed ⅝" bias through the foot directly to the needle plate, skipping the initial guide so that it will stitch the bias down the center of the tape. The result will be bias with perfect little pleats that make it much easier to lay down curved lines. Pleated bias also gives the effect of a double layer of bias when stitched and washed.

The Chenille Foot

Recently, a special foot was designed specifically for sewing continuous bias. This chenille foot has an open channel for ⅝" bias and a smaller opening below the needle for ⅜" bias. The chenille foot enables you to apply both bias widths in one step by centering the ⅜" bias on the ⅝" bias as you sew. You can also pull decorative yarn through the ⅜" opening, using a slight zigzag stitch to couch the yarn on layered bias strips in one easy step. You can also feed multiple layers of ⅝" bias through the foot.

For Easier Pleating

Stitch with pleats facing down (i.e., toward you) to avoid catching them in the ruffler foot.

demonstration
Chenille to *Dye* For

Because you are working with 100 percent natural fibers, you can do some amazing things with a little bit of dye or some textile pens. I've found two methods of dyeing that produce very different results, and we'll discuss a favorite method for giving fabrics a mellow aged look.

Dyes and Results
Whether using instant tea (*left* in photo) or liquid dyes (*right* in photo), you can achieve beautiful results with hand-dyeing plain and prepleated bias.

The "Pie Tin" Method
This method is fast and easy to do. The only equipment you need is disposable aluminum pie tins (one for water and one for each color of dye you'll be working with) and any kind of dye that is suitable for natural fibers. I prefer liquid dyes because they are readily available and simple to use without a lot of preparation. Heat-set dyes work perfectly for chenille as well. (A heat-set dye becomes colorfast and permanent with the application of heat, either by an iron or in the dryer.)

White, natural and any color bias light enough to pick up a darker color can be overdyed with this technique.

1 Protect your work space with a plastic drop cloth or trash bag, or use an old vinyl tablecloth. Be sure to wear plastic gloves and an apron to protect your clothing.

2 Fill a pie pan with enough water to cover the bottom of the pan (about ¾" [19mm]).

A Word of Caution

Never use cooking items for dyeing projects. Designate pans, spoons, bowls and other utensils as dyeing tools only, and store them away from any area where food is prepared.

3 Work a roll of ⅝" bias with your hands, pulling and bending the sides to loosen the layers so they aren't so tight (especially toward the center). Place the loosened bias roll flat side down in the water-filled pie pan. Soak the roll, then turn and soak the other side until the roll is fully saturated.

The Pie Tin Approach to Dyeing

When a roll of continuous bias is laid flat in dye (*left*), the edges absorb the color, producing an interesting tinged effect (see bias in the upper center).

4 Using a separate pie tin for each color of dye, mix water and dye in the bottom to a depth of about ¼" (6mm). (For a softer color, add more water.)

5 Remove the soaked bias roll from the water-filled pie tin and dip it, flat side down, in the dye-filled tin. The longer the roll remains in the dye, the deeper the dye penetrates the bias. The outside edges might make it appear the bias roll has completely absorbed the dye, but as you unwind the roll you'll find that only the edges of the bias are dyed.

6 Turn the bias roll over and dip again; or, for a different effect, dip the other side of the roll in a new color.

7 Remove the dyed roll carefully to avoid dripping or splashing. Place on a foam plate or on multiple layers of paper towels with a protective plastic sheet underneath.

   Allow the roll to air-dry for several days. The dry roll of bias with its vibrantly colored edges will be ready to use for any of the projects in this book.

Sponge Dye Randomly

Don't be afraid to experiment as you sponge on the dye. A random approach can produce delightful results.

Bunch-and-Sponge Method

For a more mottled or tie-dyed effect, try the bunch-and-sponge approach. You'll need heat-set dye, a pie tin or plastic disposable bowl for each color of dye you plan to use and a piece of cellulose scrubbing sponge or a 1" (25mm) sponge brush for each color.

   Unroll the bias into shallow piles on a table covered with plastic sheeting. You can work on several yards of bias at a time; if you have room to spread out, you can unroll even more. For more vibrant color results, dampen the mounds of bias with a spritz of water.

   Pour a small amount of liquid heat-set dye into the bottom of a pie tin. Moisten the sponge with clear water until just damp. Dip a corner of the sponge into the dye and blot randomly onto the pile of bias. Work with one color or multiple colors of dye as desired (be sure to change sponges for each color).

   Turn the mound of bias over occasionally, move it around to redistribute it and blot on more color until you're pleased with the result. Line dry the finished bias—do *not* throw the bias in the dryer.

   If you're not satisfied with the appearance of the dried bias, repeat the process as many times as you wish, adding more color and moving the bias around until you're happy with the final effect.

Tea-Dyeing Bias

Tea-dyeing is a popular method of aging textiles. All you need for your *dye* is a jar of instant tea. The amount of tea you use will determine how deep the antiquing effect will be.

To tea-dye bias, lace and other trims, immerse yardage in a bath of ¼ cup (59ml) instant tea mixed in about a quart (1l) of warm water. Check the results regularly—if the yardage stays in the tea bath too long, the results may be darker than you wish. However, note that the yardage will dry lighter than it appears when wet (yardage should be line dried). It's better to err on the side of caution and remove the yardage sooner rather than later. If the results are too light when the yardage dries, simply reimmerse in the tea bath.

For a large item (like a jacket), use a bucket-sized container half filled with water and add tea according to the intensity of the color you want.

Another Approach to Hand-Dyeing

The flecks of color in this chenille latticework were achieved by hand-coloring a finished scarf with textile pens after the scarf was washed (but before it was dry). This scarf is featured in the Gallery in Chapter Four (page 100).

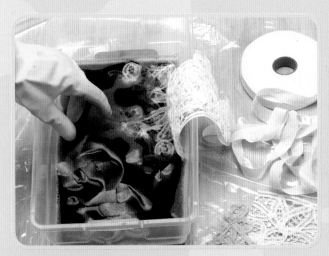

Gauging Results

The samples in the lower right corner contrast the difference between plain and tea-dyed Battenburg lace. The tea-dyed lace is still wet; the color will lighten as the lace dries.

Layered Color

A close-up of the trim on the denim purse in this chapter's Gallery (page 26) reveals the layers of color created by hand-dyeing and pleating the bias.

Gallery

One hundred percent natural fabrics are used to create a fabric very similar to old-fashioned chenille bedspreads. In the traditional chenille technique, the fabrics are layered, channel quilted together on the bias and slashed between the lines of stitching. Washing and drying the finished garment results in a soft, luxurious texture.

Hand-dyed ⅝" bias makes a wonderful trim when it's put through a pleater or ruffler foot. The perfect pleats add dimension to the bias, and you have the option of using the pleated bias for curved and circular designs. The pleats add detail to the bias and just a slight brushing of the edges, rather than washing, will keep the look fresh and show off the layered colors of the dyes.

One of the limitations of traditional allover chenille (i.e., stitch-and-slash) is that the entire surface of the project is solid chenille. You also are limited to chevron and straight lines because you must sew on the true bias for perfect results.

By using rolls or strips of continuous bias, you can break the rules of traditional chenille and go anywhere with your design. Add a little or a lot of bias, and use multiple colors and widths on one project. The possibilities are simply endless.

Chapter Two

Transforming Ready-to-Wear

Working with ready-to-wear clothing lets you skip all of the work of constructing a garment; you can jump right into the fun of adding lots of detail and embellishment.

Ready-to-wear doesn't have to mean *new*. Your closet may be full of possibilities. You can take something that is inexpensive or about to be discarded from your wardrobe and turn it into a high fashion favorite.

A thrift store or secondhand shop is a terrific source for everything from jackets and vests to skirts and accessories—even children's clothing. Look for pieces that have nice styling and open areas for design work. Denim is always a favorite, not to mention the popular sweatshirt, easy to transform into a jacket, vest and more. Remember the vintage racks, too.

Don't be afraid to change the style of a garment before you embellish it. It's easy to adjust a sleeve or shorten a jacket to make it more your style. Alter a larger size, add inserts to a smaller size or use such garments as "parts" for other projects. Be aware of fabrics and look for brand names.

If you need inspiration, browse the high-end catalogs or explore the designer departments at the mall. Movies, TV and the Internet are great sources for ideas, too.

Using multiple techniques adds interest. Pay attention to the details—a unique finishing touch makes all the difference.

Materials list

Garment
- Ready-to-wear plain denim jacket with buttons removed

Continuous Bias
- ⅝" bias (measure the design lines you want to accent on the jacket, multiply by 2 and add at least 1 yard [1m])

Additional Tools & Materials
- Replacement buttons of choice (rhinestone, vintage, hand-painted)

Simple Denim Do-Over Jacket

Let's start with the basics—and what could be more of a wardrobe basic than a denim jacket? The typical look is all metal buttons and lots of topstitching, but we'll soon change that!

The edges of a ready-to-wear jacket are already finished, which saves time and effort. The easiest way to embellish a jacket is to follow the design lines, including seams, pockets and yoke. Study your jacket for other details.

For this jacket, use heavier sewing machine needles made especially for working with denim (or use a size 90 needle).

instructions

Remove the buttons from the denim jacket. Pliers work well for taking the backs off the buttons.

1 Stitch a double layer of ⅝" bias (using a 2.0 stitch length) all the way around the edges of the jacket, aligning the edge of the bias with the jacket edge.

2 Sew bias to the pocket flaps, starting with the sides.

3 Stitch bias from 1 flap corner to the point, trimming the bias on an angle so the edge aligns with the other edge of the flap.

4 Reposition the bias at the point, aligning the angled end with the first flap edge. Stitch to the other corner. Trim even with the side of the flap.

5 Wash and dry the jacket. Sew on new or vintage buttons of your choice.

Materials list

Garment
- Ready-to-wear plain denim jacket with buttons removed

Fabric
- Decorator fabric for appliqués (enough yardage to provide at least 2 small and 1 medium motif)
- 1 vintage lace-edged hand towel or pillowcase (lace trim should be long enough to stretch across the back yoke of the jacket)

Continuous Bias
- 7 yards (6.4m) ⅜" bias (natural)

Additional Tools & Materials
- Text panel (machine-embroidered or handwritten with a textile pen)
- 3–4 dozen heat-set crystals (colors to accent appliqué colors)
- Heat-set applicator
- Mismatched vintage buttons (equal to the number of buttons removed from the jacket)

Stop and Smell the Roses Jacket

I believe you can't have too many altered denim jackets. This is one of my favorites, featuring a few of my favorite things: roses, vintage lace, some bling and, of course, some chenille!

You can use decorator and vintage fabrics to create the rough-cut appliqués on this jacket. For this project, use heavier sewing machine needles made especially for working with denim (or use a size 90 needle).

1 Create and apply rough-cut appliqués before sewing the continuous bias.

Trim the desired motifs from vintage or designer fabric, leaving about ¼" (6mm) all the way around. Like continuous bias, this extra fabric will bloom after washing, creating textured edges.

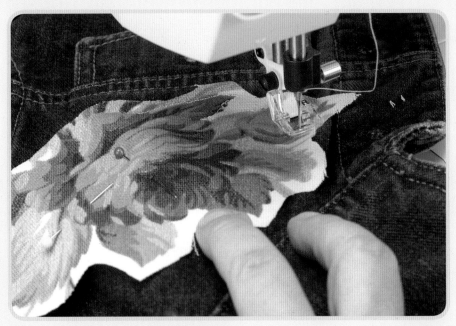

2 Pin the appliqués into place on the jacket and stitch around the outline of each design. (For free-motion sewing, use a clear embroidery free-motion foot. Keep pins away from the edge.) Drop the feed dogs so you can move the fabric wherever you want; on older sewing machines, use a darning foot.

When each appliqué is stitched securely, remove the pins.

3 Load your machine with embroidery thread. Use a color that blends but will still stand out against the detailed background of the appliqués.

Double-check to make sure the pins have been removed. Stitch details of each appliqué design. (For instance, in the project example, follow the contours of the roses.) This additional stitching will give a quilted effect and add dimension to the appliqué.

5 Brush the edges of the appliqué to bring out the texture.

4 Clip into the corners and short curves of the appliqué designs right up to the stitch line.

6 Sew a double layer of ⅜" bias along all edges and design lines of the jacket.

Creating a Text Panel

I machine-embroidered the text panel for the project jacket. However, if you don't have an embroidery machine (or an embroidery function on your sewing machine), create a panel using a textile paint pen to write out the words on a scrap of fabric. (Follow manufacturer's instructions for the pen). You could also hand-embroider the panel or cross-stitch the letters on counted thread fabric.

7 Position the text panel on the jacket (leave the edges of the panel raw); pin the panel into place. Stitch about ¼" (6mm) in from the raw edge using a feather stitch or any decorative stitch of your choice. Brush the raw edges of the panel to bring out the texture.

Sources for Vintage Lace

Look for vintage tea towels with lace edging at flea markets, rummage sales and garage sales. The width of a tea towel just about fits on the back of a jacket, and the ends of the lace will be finished. Leave about 1" (25mm) of fabric when trimming lace from a towel.

8 Trim the lace from a tea towel or pillowcase, leaving about 1" (25mm) of raw-edged fabric above the stitch line. Position the lace so the shortest part hits the yoke, covering the seam.

Sew the lace to the back of the jacket using a regular straight stitch; if the ends are raw, turn them under. Stitch across the top edge ⅛" (3mm) from the raw edge. Brush the edge for texture.

Using a Heat-Set Applicator

Heat-set applicators are available in most fabric and craft stores. They have different sized heads for picking up a variety of embellishments, including pearls, studs and crystals. Follow manufacturer's instructions for both the embellishments and the heat-set applicator.

1. Plug in the heat-set applicator and allow it to warm up for a couple of minutes.

2. Spread crystals, right side up, on the work surface. Pick up a crystal with the head of the heat-set applicator. Hold 7–10 seconds until the adhesive on the back of the crystal bubbles.

3. Place the crystal where you want it on the design by pressing down and lifting the head of the applicator. Repeat until the design is embellished as desired.

9 Embellish the rough-cut appliqués with heat-set crystals (see instructions *left*).

10 Wash and dry the jacket or brush the bias to bring up the texture. Sew on mismatched vintage buttons.

Finished Jacket Back
This gorgeous altered garment has plenty of color, texture and detail, front and back.

Child's Play Denim Jacket

Clothing for children is all about the details. A little embroidery and a little lace gives this miniature denim jacket the finishing touch. And—children love the soft texture of chenille!

Materials list

Garment
- Plain child's denim jacket (new or used)

Continuous Bias
- 3–5 yards (2.7–4.6m) ⅜" bias (pale pink)

Additional Tools & Materials
- Purchased iron-on embroidered appliqué*
  *NOTE: Not needed if you plan to machine-embroider a design directly to the back of the jacket.
- 2–3 yards (1.8–2.7m) narrow white trim (may need more or less depending on jacket size)

instructions

1 If you wish to embellish the jacket with machine embroidery, do this before applying the bias. Use a design and stitches of your choice.

  If you don't have an embroidery machine, take a look at the prestitched embroidered appliqués that are available at most fabric stores or online.

3 Stitch ⅜"pale pink bias (using a 1.5 stitch length) to the jacket, aligning the bias along the straight edge of the lace. The center of the bias should be positioned over the last row of stitching on the lace.

4 Use a wire chenille brush to lift and fluff the fibers to create the chenille texture, or you can spritz the sewn bias with water and throw the jacket in the dryer. You can also put the jacket through a regular wash cycle and dry.

A Thrifty Source for Jackets

I have found thrift stores to be a great resource for plain, unembellished denim jackets for children as well as adults.

2 Stitch narrow lace to the jacket along the flat seam lines using a 2.5 stitch length.

Extra Fullness

To give your chenille a fuller look, lay down two layers of continuous bias.

Little Looper Scarf

A fringe frame (also known as a hairpin lace frame or a Loop-dee-Doodle™) can be used to make luxuriant textured looped fringe for embellishing apparel and accessories as well as a fashionable scarf. Looped fringe also adds pizzazz to the *Velour Couture Jacket and Bag* (page 41).

Materials list

Continuous Bias
- 25 yards (23m) ⅜" bias (color of choice)

Additional Tools & Materials
- 25 yards (23m) decorative yarn* (color that works well with the continuous bias) *NOTE: Yarn with lots of texture works best.*
- Fringe frame (traditional hairpin lace frame or a Loop-dee-Doodle™)

1 Hold the ends of prestitched ⅜" bias and yarn against the sidebar of the fringe frame and pin into place. Wrap the bias and yarn around the frame until 5–6" (13–15cm) have been wrapped, then place the frame on the sewing machine bed under the needle, positioned to stitch down the center of the wrapped bias and yarn.

2 Starting with a backstitch over the bias and loops, sew ⅜" bias down the middle of the wrapped bias and yarn using a 1.0 stitch. As you fill the frame, move the loops down and continue to wind bias and yarn and stitch the bias down the center. (The closer together the loops are on the frame, the fuller the scarf will be.)

   When you've created the desired length for your scarf, finish with a backstitch over the bias.

3 Remove the looped scarf from the fringe frame. Wash and dry to make it bloom.

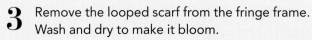

Bias for Stability

Sewing ⅜" bias down the center of the loops on the frame instead of stitching on the loops themselves gives the scarf extra stability. When making fringe that will be sewn as trim to a garment or other project, water-soluble stabilizer is stitched down the middle of the loops instead of bias (see *Velour Couture Jacket and Bag*, page 41). The base fabric and extra stitching reinforce the fringe so the additional bias isn't necessary.

Velour Couture Jacket and Bag

My favorite part of transforming ready-to-wear is to start with a garment with one use and transform it into something with a whole new life.

A velour running jacket is a perfect example—wear the altered version for an evening out (and take along a matching bag made from the jacket's hood).

Materials list

Garment
- Velour activewear jacket with hood

Continuous Bias
- 40 yards (37m) ⅜" bias (color that compliments jacket color)

Additional Tools & Materials
- Fringe frame (hairpin lace frame or Loop-dee-Doodle™)
- 40 yards (37m) decorative yarn (this yardage is adequate for most jacket sizes)
- ¾"-wide (19mm) strip of fabric-like water-soluble stabilizer equal to the length of the neckline and both front edges of your jacket plus 2" (5cm)
- ¾"-wide (19mm) strip of fabric-like water-soluble stabilizer equal to the circumference of the top of the bag plus 2" (5cm)

instructions

1 Cut the hood off the sweatshirt; be careful not to cut into the finished edge at the neckline.

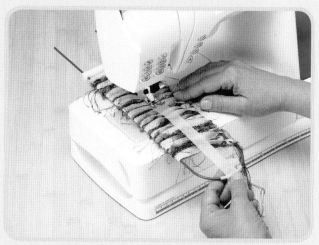

3 Cut a ¾"(19mm) strip of fabric-like water-soluble stabilizer the length of the jacket neckline and front edges plus 2" (5cm). Slip this strip under the needle so it lies down the center of the wrapped bias and yarn on the frame.

2 Hold the ends of prestitched ⅜" bias and yarn against the sidebar of the fringe frame. Wrap the bias and yarn around the frame until 5–6" (13–15cm) have been wrapped, then place the frame on the sewing machine bed under the needle, positioned to stitch down the center of the wrapped bias and yarn.

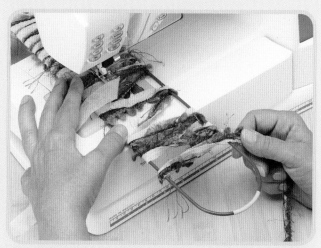

4 Stitch down the center of the stabilizer over the wrapped bias and yarn. Move the unstitched portion of the stabilizer to the side and push the stitched bias/yarn loops down on the frame.

Wrap more bias and yarn, reposition the stabilizer and continue to stitch. (The closer together the loops are on the frame, the fuller the fringe will be.)

5 Stitch the loomed trim to the jacket, starting at the bottom of the zipper and continuing up the front of the jacket, around the neckline and down the other front side. Place the edge of the water-soluble strip next to the zipper's edge so the loomed trim is positioned about ⅜" (10mm) in. Pin the trim in place or stitch as you go.

8 Sew the cut edge of the hood as a side seam, stitching a ¼" (6mm) seam up to, but not over, the casing. Sew back over the raw edge with a zigzag stitch (use a fairly wide stitch length such as 4.5).

6 Embellish the jacket with heat-set crystals as desired (see instructions on page 36).

9 Use the hood's drawstring to close the bag or insert cord or dyed ribbon.

10 Embellish the bag as desired: with looped fringe, heat-set crystals and/or rough-cut appliqués.

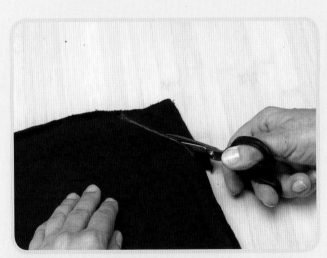

7 To create a bag from the hood, mark to round the corners, then trim.

Materials list

Garment

- Black crewneck pullover sweatshirt

Fabric

- 10" × 12" (25cm × 30cm) coordinated cotton Fabric A (jacket-back collage)
- 8½" × 7½" (22cm × 19cm) coordinated cotton Fabric B (jacket-back collage)
- ¾ yard (69cm) Fabric C (using lengthwise grain, front jacket panel)
- ⅜ yard (34cm) Fabric C (using crosswise grain, front jacket panel)
- Decorator fabric (enough yardage to provide 2 small, 2 medium and 1 large appliqué)

Continuous Bias

- 40 yards (37m) ⅝" bias (black)
- 25 yards (23m) ⅜" bias (khaki)

Additional Tools & Materials

- 7" × 7½" (18cm × 19cm) image panel (jacket-back collage)
- 20 yards (18m) coordinated textured yarn
- Temporary spray adhesive or water-soluble fabric glue stick
- Heat-set crystals
- Heat-set applicator
- 1 button (closure)

The "No Way It's a Sweatshirt!" Jacket

I know that the pullover sweatshirt has been done and overdone, but this jacket has something new to *say* about that, featuring a personalized layered back panel and unique details.

With some new twists to a few of my favorite techniques, you can make a jacket that leaves the whole sweatshirt concept far behind.

instructions

1 Trim the bottom and cuffs from the sweatshirt and cut an opening up the front of the shirt.

2 At the neckline, turn down the corner of the cut edge and stitch into place. This further stabilizes the cut edge for sewing on the continuous bias.

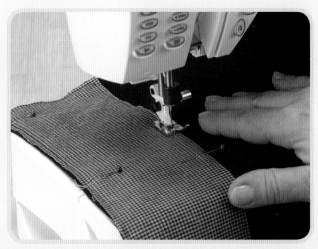

3 Cut a panel from print Fabric C that's 4" (10cm) wide and several inches longer than the length of the jacket front (there should be at least 5" [13cm] of extra fabric at the top of the panel). Affix the panel to the front of the jacket along 1 side of the cut opening (instead of pins, use either spray-on fabric adhesive or a water-soluble fabric glue stick).

Repeat for the second Fabric C panel on the other side of the cut opening.

4 Trim both panels at the bottom; at the neckline, trim just below the seam line following the contour of the banding. Stitch around the fabric panels, sewing close to the edges.

5 Zigzag stitch the raw edges all around the fabric panels to prevent fraying.

6 Sew 4 vertical rows of stitches on each panel about ¾"(19mm) from the edge and ¾" apart for a quilted effect.

8 Pin the scallop pattern in place so the bottom of the scallop aligns with the bottom edge of the jacket. Cut along the scallop pattern all the way around the bottom of the jacket.

7 To make a custom scalloped hemline pattern, cut a 4" (10cm) strip of tissue or other light-weight paper equal to the measurement of the jacket's bottom edge. Fold this strip into the width of the scallop you want.

Use something round (a saucer, bowl, tape roll, etc.) as a template. It should provide a rounded edge that fits the width of the folded paper and is 1½" (4cm) deep from the upper edge of the paper. Trace this circle edge on the folded paper and trim around the rounded bottom of the scallop. Unfold and you have your scallop pattern.

9 Create a text panel (machine-embroidered or handwritten with a fabric pen). Center the text panel, leaving enough space at the corner for an appliqué. (See instructions on page 33 for making rough-cut appliqués.) Adhere and stitch the panel and appliqué into place.

10 Cut a 10" × 12" (25cm × 30cm) panel from Fabric A and a 7½" × 8½" (19cm × 22cm) panel from Fabric B.

Create an image panel 7" × 7½" (18cm × 19cm). Layer the Fabric B panel on the Fabric A panel and the image panel on the Fabric B panel. Center this stack on the back of the jacket.

12 Create free-form swirls with pleated ⅝" bias. Work in the open spaces. Start your swirl in the center, laying the pleated bias around as the swirl grows to 3 or 4 rows. Bring the end of the bias out to a soft, curving line. Center layered ⅜" bias and yarn over ⅝" bias and stitch over the swirled pleated bias.

Make 3 smaller swirls for the side of each front fabric panel; reverse the direction of the swirls for interest.

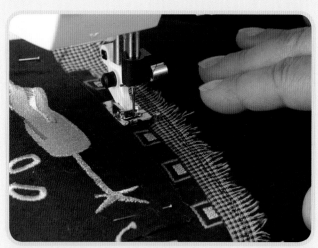

11 Pin all 3 layers into place. Stitch around each panel about ¼" (6mm) from the edge using a basic or decorative stitch (such as a blanket stitch). Leave the top panel in place but pull the edges aside to stitch the second panel.

When stitching is complete, brush the edges of the panels to bring out the texture.

Creating an Image Panel

There are a number of techniques for creating an image panel for the back of the jacket: machine embroidery, fabric photo transfer, appliqué or drawing a design with fabric pens.

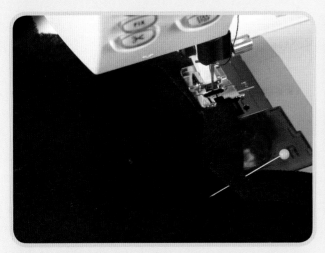

13 Stitch ⅝" bias to the wrong side of the scalloped bottom edge. Stitch to the inner point of the scallop, then flip the bias and continue to sew. Keep the edge of the bias ⅛" (3mm) beyond the raw edge.

16 Embellish the jacket as desired with new or vintage buttons and heat-set crystals. (See page 36 for instructions on using heat-set embellishments.)

14 Stitch ⅝" bias to the right side of the scalloped bottom edge, flipping the bias at the inner points of the scallops as you sew and matching the edges of the bias on the right and wrong sides of the bottom edge.

15 Center layered ⅜" bias and yarn over ⅝" bias and sew to all the edges of the jacket: scalloped bottom, neckline, cuffs and along the edges of the patterned fabric panels on the jacket front. Flip the bias at each inner scallop point before sewing down with yarn.

Ring of Flowers Skirt

Although a jacket is a natural for an embellishment project, we often overlook some of the other basics in our closet.

In this case, a simple skirt can be the canvas for something spectacular. Just watch this garden grow!

Materials list

Garment
- Plain A-line skirt

Continuous Bias
- 3 yards (2.7m)
  ⅜" bias (rose)
- 3 yards (2.7m)
  ⅜" bias (pale pink)
- 7 yards (6.4m)
  ⅜" bias (sage green)

Additional Tools & Materials
- 1¾" (4cm) lace edging, yardage equivalent to the measurement of the hemline plus 2" (5cm)
- Dressmaker's chalk
- Template for flowers (page 124)

instructions

1 With chalk, draw a line around the skirt 3½" (9cm) above the hemline. Make a mark every 3" (8cm) along the chalk line (adjust according to the circumference of skirt). At every chalk mark, draw 3" (8cm) flower stems.

2 Precut 3" (8cm) lengths of ⅜" sage green bias to use for stems and leaves (cut 2 leaves for each stem drawn on the skirt).

3 Sew a single layer of ⅜" bias over each stem line using a basic 1.5 stitch down the middle of the bias. Form 2 strips of bias into a V for leaves, flipping the bias at the point of each V. Pin the leaves ¾" (19mm) from the top and bottom of the stem, attaching at the center of the stem. Sew down the center of each leaf, pivoting at the point of the V.

4 Use 2 colors of ⅜" bias for the flowers, alternating colors for each flower (this project uses rose and pale pink).

Cut a 12" (30cm) strip of bias for each flower (each petal uses 4" [10cm] of bias). For consistently sized petals, mark with a pin every 4" (10cm).

Fold and flip the bias at the top and bottom to make each petal, pinning in place, then stitch down the center of the bias.

5 Apply a lace band around the hem to barely cover the bottoms of the flower stems.

6 Sew a strip of ⅜" sage green bias to cover the top stitch line of the lace band. Brush the edges of the chenille. Sew a button on each flower where the petals and stems meet.

Artsy Tips

For a more artsy effect:

- Avoid making the flower petals all exactly the same.

- Remember that an uneven number of items is more pleasing visually.

Diamond Details Textured Top

Yoke detailing and hemlines are perfect places for simple border designs and embellishment details. This linen top had all of the ingredients for a closet couture transformation.

Materials list

Garment
- Ready-to-wear tunic-style top (project uses a linen top)

Continuous Bias
- 13 yards (12m) ⅜" bias (natural)
  NOTE: Yardage should be adequate for most sizes.

Additional Tools & Materials
- Dressmaker's chalk
- Lace edging equal to hemline measurement plus 1" (25mm)
- Small ⅜" (10mm) buttons (for the center of every other zigzag on the front and back yoke and for every other diamond along the hemline)
- One ⅝" (16mm) button for the center front yoke detail

instructions

1 Measure the middle of the front yoke and mark with a pin.

Measure the distance from the pin to each end of the neckline, find the center and mark with a pin. (Each pin represents a bottom point of the zigzag pattern.)

2 Lay a single layer of ⅜" bias on a diagonal from the upper end of the front yoke to the first bottom point pin. Pin the bias in place, then flip the bias at the point and extend the bias up to the next pin at the neckline edge. Pin and flip the bias again. Continue across the front yoke, completing the zigzag pattern.

Repeat for the back yoke.

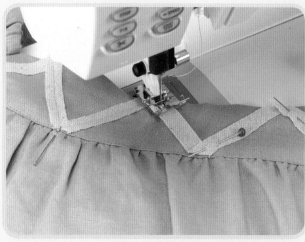

3 Using a straight 1.5 stitch, sew the bias zigzag into place across the yoke, removing the pins as you stitch.

Sew the zigzag along the back yoke in the same manner.

4 With chalk, mark a line 1" (25mm) above the tunic bottom all the way around, then mark a second line 3" (8cm) above the first line. Make a chalk mark every 1½" (4cm) across the top and bottom lines.

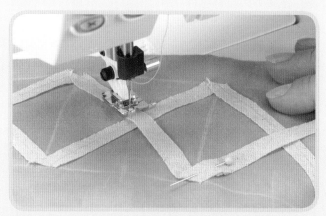

5 Draw a vertical line between every other set of 1½" (4cm) marks along the top and bottom lines. Lay down the first row of bias zigzags by starting at the top of the first vertical line on the hemline, running it to the bottom of the next vertical line. Pin into place, then flip the bias and continue to the top of the next vertical line. Continue in this manner around the bottom of the tunic.

The second row of zigzags begins at the bottom of the first vertical line. Lay the bias running to the top of the next vertical line, pin, flip the bias and continue around the bottom of the tunic.

When the border is complete, there will be a point of flipped bias at the top and bottom of each vertical line. The 1½" marks between the zigzag points provide a visual reference to where the lines of bias should intersect.

6 Using a 1.5 stitch, sew down the center of 1 line of bias zigzags all the way around the tunic; then sew the second line.

7 Cut prestitched ⅜" bias into 3" (8cm) strips, 2 strips for each small rosette. (A small rosette goes into the center of every other zigzag along the neckline and in the center of every other diamond along the hem.)

Fold a bias strip so the ends overlap. Fold another strip in the same manner and layer 1 folded strip of bias over the other to create a cross shape.

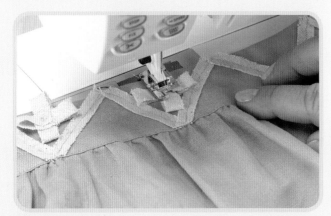

8 With a 3.5 zigzag stitch (0 length), attach the rosette to the center of a zigzag or diamond, sewing down and across the center of the rosette. Add a small button to each rosette center. (In addition to being decorative, this helps secure the rosette.)

Repeat for each small rosette needed to complete the pattern, top and bottom.

9 Cut a 16"(41cm) strip of prestitched ⅜" bias to create a large rosette. Hold the end of the bias strip and make a loop, catching the loop at the center of the rosette. Pin the first loop, then continue looping and pinning the bias. The loops should radiate from the center, longer at the top, bottom and side points, and shorter in between.

Sew the large rosette just below the middle zigzag point along the front neckline. Stitch at the center of the rosette, catching the ends of the bias. Embellish the center with a button.

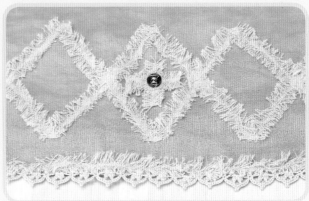

10 Stitch lace along the bottom of the tunic so the edging extends beyond the hemline. Sew a single layer of ⅜" bias so the stitching runs along the top edge of the lace.

11 When finished, wash and dry the top or brush for a fringed look.

Gallery

This bias cut skirt has godet insets perfect for the placement of an individual chenille and appliqué design. I applied the flower petals to the skirt using paper-backed fusible web, then stitched them into place before edging them with ³⁄₈" continuous bias. The stems and leaves are also a single layer of ³⁄₈" bias.

A trip to the discount store is a perfect place to find great jackets and vests that turn into designer pieces with a little bit of time and embellishment. Textured machine appliqués and swirls of prepleated ⁵⁄₈" hand-dyed bias are the finishing touches that give this standout its personality. Brushing the pleated bias instead of washing it gives the detailing even more dimension and interest.

Using ⅜" prestitched bias, I stitched 4" (10cm) loops around the outside edge of this handbag. Adding ⅜" bias between the rows of decorative stitching makes the stitching stand out. Figure-eight flower designs occupy the diamond intersections.

Continuous bias also makes it easier and faster to finish edges, raw seams and the strap without bulk.

The plain sweatshirt is an ideal base for adding machine-embroidered snowflakes and heat-set pearls. The fringed ⅜" bias and textured yarn trim around the neckline take this sweatshirt jacket to the next level. The bag is the perfect recycling project for the discarded hood, a gorgeous match for this fabulous jacket.

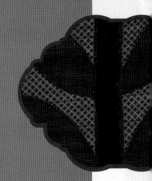

Chapter Three

Recapturing Vintage Style

What could be better than a touch of chenille to give a project that vintage look? I remember sitting on my grandmother's bedspread and studying the lines of chenille and the patterns and colors of the soft tufts that made the bedspread so inviting. My grandmother even had a robe that was covered with interwoven patterns of chenille.

Recent years have brought a resurgence of this style, but with a new look and applications that allow us to use chenille in ways it's never been used before. Though still a natural for home decorator projects, don't limit chenille to the bedroom. Give any project a vintage look by finishing the edges with chenille or using chenille as an embellishment.

It can be fun to use a vintage apron pattern from the 1930s or 1940s and add a chenille edge or design. Type *chenille* into the search field of an online auction and check out the vintage chenille items for sale. These old chenille bedspreads are a great inspiration for your next project with continuous bias. You will be amazed how easily these designs can be reproduced, so use them for everything from pillows to jackets and more. Replace outdated colors with something bright, and stitch the designs onto an unexpected base fabric that will bring it into the twenty-first century.

Materials list

Fabric

- Half apron (ready-made) *or* fabric for apron* as determined by pattern
- Purchased plain pot holder *or* two 7" × 7" (18cm × 18cm) squares of fabric*

Continuous Bias

- 10 yards (9m) ⅝" bias (wine)
- ½ yard (46cm) prepleated ⅝" bias (sage)
- ½ yard (46cm) pre-pleated ⅝" bias (wine)
- 10" (25cm) ⅜" bias (dark green)

Additional Tools & Materials

- Apron pattern of choice* (project is designed for a rounded apron)
- Pot holder pattern of choice* (project uses a 7" × 7" pot holder)
- 7" × 7" heat-resistant fleece interfacing*
- Templates for scallop and pocket, pattern for cherry design (page 122)
  NOTE: Needed only if making apron or pot holder from scratch.

Vintage Apron with Pot Holder

Aprons have become very popular again, and this one has vintage flair that makes it a standout. Make the apron from scratch using a favorite pattern or restyle a ready-made apron. (The project is designed for an apron with a rounded shape.) Touches of chenille will give it a whole new look.

Make a matching pot holder from your apron fabric, or use a complimentary fabric if your apron is ready-made.

instructions

1 Make 2 photocopies of the scallop template on page 122 (enlarge as indicated) and cut out. Fold 1 of the scallop templates in half.

2 Starting at the bottom right edge of the apron, align the long, straight side of the folded template along the apron edge; the bottom of the scallop should align with bottom edge of the apron.

Align the full scallop template next to the half template; mark the scallops from both templates. Continue around the curved edge, matching the corner of the full template to the marked scallop and making sure the bottom of the template is aligned with the bottom edge of the apron. Mark each scallop.

Cut out the scallops and zigzag stitch over the raw scalloped edge of the apron.

3 Sew a single layer of ⅝" bias to the underside of the apron along the scalloped edge. (See page 48 for instructions on sewing bias to a scalloped edge.)

The bias should extend about ⅛" (3mm) beyond the zigzagged edge.

4 On the top side of the apron, sew a double layer of ⅝" bias.

5 Photocopy the pocket template on page 122 (enlarge as indicated) and cut the pocket from the apron fabric.

Stitch ¼" (6mm) from the edge of the pocket. Turn the raw edge to the wrong side of the pocket, fold along the stitched line and press.

Zigzag stitch across the raw top edge of the pocket with the inverted scallop. Sew a single layer of ⅝" bias to the top edge of the wrong side of the pocket, then sew a double layer of ⅝" bias along the upper edge of the pocket on the right side.

6 Position the pocket to the apron as shown in the photo on page 58 or as desired. Pin the pocket in place. Topstitch along the fold.

7 If you're making your apron from a pattern rather than using a ready-made, sew the waistband and ties as instructed.

8 Whatever type of apron you're embellishing, sew a double layer of ⅝" bias along the seam at the base of the waistband.

10 Photocopy or trace the cherry pattern on page 122 and transfer to 1 side of the pot holder. Stitch a single layer of ⅜" bias over the stem lines, flipping the bias at the point of the stems' V.

Pin pleated ⅜" bias to the cherry outlines and continue winding the bias into the center like a spiral and stitching to fill in the space.

9 If you're making a pot holder from a pattern, construct and sew according to pattern directions.

Chenille Effects: Fringed or Fluffy

On small projects, chenille can be brushed for a fringed effect. For a fluffier look, spritz the chenille with water and machine-dry the project.

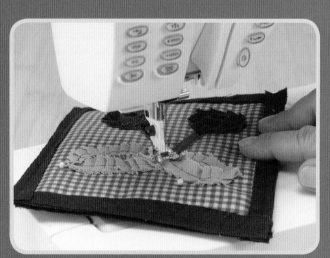

11 Shape a 12" (30cm) length of ⅝" pleated bias into a figure-eight at the top of the stem, flipping the bias at each leaf point. Pin and sew into place on either side of the stem end.

12 Sew a large vintage button to the waistband for the pot holder.

Sunflower Apron

I love sunflowers and I love aprons. This vintage-style design is perfect for entertaining and will definitely be a conversation piece.

Materials list

Fabric

- Purchased denim or canvas chef's apron (available in craft stores and cooking supply stores)
- ⅝ yards (0.6m) gold print Fabric A (sunflower head)
- ⅝ yard (0.6m) dark print Fabric B (sunflower stem and lower 2 leaf sets)
- ⅝ yard (0.6m) dark print Fabric C (sunflower pocket, upper 2 leaf sets and apron bottom panel)

Continuous Bias

- 3 yards (2.7m) ⅜" bias (dark brown)
- 1 yard (1m) prepleated ⅝" bias (dark brown)

Additional Tools & Materials

- Paper-backed fusible web
- Contrasting thread for decorative stitching
- 2½ yards (2.3m) 1¼"-wide (3cm) ribbon (apron ties)
- Templates for the sunflower head appliqué, sunflower leaves appliqué and the apron pocket (page 123)

instructions

1 Wash the apron to preshrink it. Cut off the ties at the binding edge (ribbons will replace the ties).

2 Trace the templates for the appliqué pieces on page 123 onto fusible web. Also draw a 1" × 8" (2.5cm × 20cm) stem on the fusible web. Iron to fuse the web to the wrong side of Fabric A (sunflower head), Fabric B (sunflower stem, pocket and 2 sets of leaves) and Fabric C (2 sets of leaves). Cut out each appliqué piece along the tracing line.

3 Cut a fabric panel 9" (23cm) deep from Fabric C and shape it to fit the bottom edge of the apron up to the binding. Pin into place.

4 Stitch the panel to the apron. Run a zigzag stitch, blanket (hemming) stitch or other decorative stitch around all the edges of the panel.

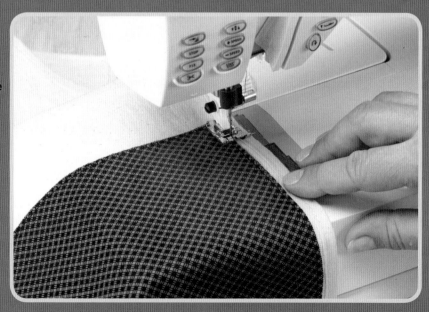

Get Creative with Stitches

Review the utility stitches on your sewing machine. Many can serve as decorative stitches as well (such as the hemming stitch, which looks like the blanket stitch used in hand embroidery).

5 Sew rows of straight stitches across the fabric panel; start ¾" (19mm) from the top edge and sew rows ¾" apart.

Quilting the Fabric Panel

Sewing ¾" (19mm) rows of stitching on wide decorative panels gives your project a quilted effect when washed. It also keeps the fabric panel smooth and professional looking.

6 Remove the paper backing from the appliqué pieces. Iron to fuse the pieces into place (see photo on page 61 for placement); start with the flower stem followed by the sunflower head, then the leaf sets.

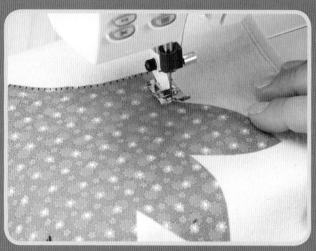

7 When all appliqué pieces are fused, run a zigzag stitch over the raw edges of the entire flower, stem and leaves.

8 Use the template on page 123 to cut out 2 pocket pieces from Fabric C. Iron fusible webbing to the wrong side of each piece, then iron to fuse the 2 pieces together.
  Zigzag stitch over the raw edges of the fused pocket piece all the way around.

9 Sew pleated ⅝" bias along the bottom edge of the pocket, starting and ending just beyond the top edge to cover. Bias also should cover the zigzag stitch around the rest of the pocket. Continue to sew curved rows of pleated bias, filling in the pocket to create the sunflower head.

10 Sew pleated ⅝" bias up the center of the stem.

12 Sew one 23" (58cm) length of ribbon to the 2 top corners of the apron for the neck loop. Sew two 31" (79cm) lengths of ribbon to each side of the waist for the back ties. *NOTE: Adjust the length of the neck loop ribbon for a better fit, if necessary.*

11 Sew the pocket to the top center of the flower appliqué piece by stitching along the center of the first row of pleated bias.

13 Sew ⅜" bias along the entire edge of the apron. The edge of the bias should align with the inner edge of the binding.

Wash or brush the chenille to fluff it.

Vintage Pillow

When I think of chenille, I think of my grandmother and her soft, colorful bedspread. Working with continuous bias makes it possible to reproduce such memories with new projects like this great vintage-style chenille pillow top.

Finished size: 16" × 16" (14cm × 14cm).

Materials list

Fabric
- 17" × 17" (43cm × 43cm) medium weight Fabric A, preshrunk (pillow top)
- Two 17" × 20" (43cm × 51cm) lighter weight coordinating Fabric B, preshrunk (pillow back)

Continuous Bias
- 3 yards (2.7m) ⅜" bias (rose)
- 20 yards (18.3m) ⅝" bias (jade)

Additional Tools & Materials
- 17" × 17" (43cm × 43cm) fabric-like water- soluble stabilizer
- 16" × 16"(41cm × 41cm) pillow form
- Design template for pillow (page 124)

instructions

1 Photocopy the design template on page 124, enlarging as indicated.

2 Cut a piece of water-soluble stabilizer to size and place over the enlarged design template. Trace the pattern onto the water-soluble stabilizer.

3 Cut a 17" × 17" (43cm × 43cm) piece of Fabric A for the pillow top. Zigzag stitch around the edges of the square to prevent fraying.

4 Position and pin the traced stabilizer to the right side of the fabric.

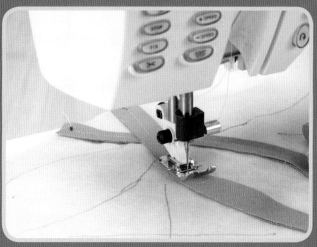

5 Using a 2.0 stitch length, sew a double layer of jade ⅝" bias centered over the traced pattern lines. The bias will intersect, following a curving figure-eight pattern.

6 Sew the flower portion of the design with a double layer of rose ⅜" bias. Each leg of the X runs up the middle of each petal. Starting at the center of the flower, sew bias along 1 leg of the X, flip the bias at the point to form a loop, then sew down the other side of the petal. Continue to sew along the opposite leg of the X in the same fashion, forming a figure-eight over 1 half of the X.

Repeat for the other half of the X, creating a figure-eight and ending in the center.

7 Cut two 17" × 20" (43cm × 51cm) pieces of Fabric B for the pillow back. Fold each piece in half to create two 17" × 10" (43cm × 25cm) pieces.

9 Finish the pillow edges with chenille (see page 21 for the techniques, including instructions on tapering corners).

8 Lay the pillow top right side down with the 2 folded pieces on top, raw edges on the outside and the folds in the Fabric B pieces overlapping in the center.

Stitch the pillow top and back pieces together, sewing ¼" (6mm) from the pillow edge all around. Next, zigzag stitch (with a 4.0 stitch length) over the pillow edges.

10 Wash and dry the pillow top, or simply fluff the chenille with a wire brush. Insert the pillow form through the flap in the back.

Materials list

Fabric

- Yardage as specific by jacket pattern*

  NOTE: Most jackets and sizes will require 2 yards (1.8m).

Continuous Bias

- 70 yards (64m)**
  ⅝" bias (natural)

- 35 yards (32m)**
  ⅜" bias (natural)

  **NOTE: Yardage may vary according to jacket style and size.*

Additional Tools & Materials

- Jacket pattern of choice (with simple lines)

- 60"-wide (1.5m) fabric-like water-soluble stabilizer (same yardage as fabric for selected pattern)***

  ***NOTE: Most jackets and sizes will require 2 yards (1.8m).*

- Wash-away marking pen

- Vintage buttons (enough for the center of each flower)

- Design template for jacket (page 124)

Vintage-Style Jacket

Take your favorite vintage chenille design and apply it to a jacket or vest for an instant fashion showstopper.

This jacket repeats the same motif used in the *Vintage Pillow* on page 65 but replaces colored bias with natural for a rich monochromatic look.

instructions

1 Trace the pieces of your jacket pattern onto water-soluble stabilizer and cut out, allowing an extra ½" (13mm) all around on each pattern piece.

4 Finish the edges of the jacket with ⅝" bias (see page 21 for detailed instructions). Use a single layer of bias on the wrong side of the jacket and double-layered bias on the right side.

2 Trace the same design template (page 124) that you used for the *Vintage Pillow* (page 65) onto the water-soluble pattern pieces, repeating the design where necessary to cover each piece. Make sure the design on the front pieces match.

5 Wash and dry the jacket. Sew vintage buttons to the centers of the flowers.

3 Stitch a single layer of ⅝" bias to the design lines for the long figure-eight repeats, then sew ⅜" bias in loops to the Xs to form flowers. (See the *Vintage Pillow* directions on page 66 for details of this technique.)

Button Hunt

It's not necessary to have matching buttons on the jacket. Raid your button box for old and unique buttons or scavenge them from thrift store clothing. Jars and tins of buttons are usually available at flea markets and antique malls. Mother of pearl buttons are a great choice for this project.

Gallery

One of the charms of true vintage chenille is that many of the pieces use multiple layers and interesting designs.

For this jacket, I cut the pattern pieces from medium-weight cotton and laid down the base design with a single layer of ⅜" dark brown bias. Once the background chenille was stitched into place, the flowers and vines were added in contrasting colors.

When the jacket was completed, washed and dried, the added designs popped to the surface, creating the look of vintage chenille but with a high fashion style and feel.

Aprons have become a fashion statement! This one reproduces the style of a vintage apron, but the elegant machine embroidery and chenille accents turn it into an elegant accessory for any party or gathering.

Soft, cuddly chenille is perfect for children's clothing. Children love the inviting texture, and moms love the fact that chenille is washable!

A vintage diamond design takes minutes to stitch into place on the body and hood of this toddler's jacket. The sleeves are simply a double layer of the cotton fabric used for the jacket body, quilted together in a diamond design using a decorative stitch. The edges are finished with the same ⅝" bias used for the allover design, which makes the jacket fast and easy to complete.

The base of this vest is recycled jeans embellished with bits and pieces of vintage linens, laces and trims. To frame and set off the panels, I used ⅜" continuous bias as an outline and to highlight individual detailing. Finishing the outer edges and the armhole edges with ⅝" bias embellishes while doing away with the need for facings and hems, eliminating bulk.

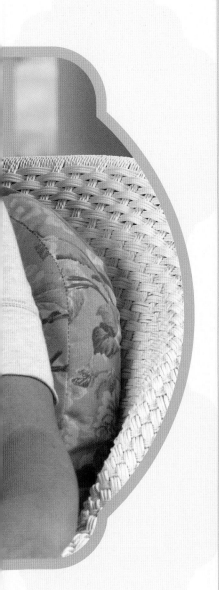

Chapter Four

Working with Unexpected Materials

I've had more fun doing research and development with continuous bias than anything else I've ever done in my sewing room. Playing and experimenting with bias is only part of it; there's also exploring the various base fabrics.

Testing new fabrics and techniques is the part of creating texture that I enjoy the most. I like to push the envelope! I began stitching continuous bias onto materials that seemed unlikely to succeed, and I was amazed when things that shouldn't work, did.

One of my first experiments was stitching bias onto water-soluble stabilizer. I began with simple projects like scarves (see page 80) and was so excited about the knit-like results that I began making entire jackets (see page 83) on this wash-away base. I found that I could make even chenille "lace" on water-soluble stabilizer (see page 86).

I prefer to keep my jackets lightweight and soft, therefore I use base fabrics that have a nice drape and give a flattering look. What could be lighter than lace? The combination of chenille and lace was a perfect match! The lace I used for my "practice" piece was an old, stained tablecloth from my linen closet (I like to experiment with things I won't feel badly about if the project doesn't work). The finished jacket had a vintage look that I hadn't expected, and a "tea bath" gave it true Victorian charm (see page 74).

A search of your fabric and embellishment stash may bring up items from the 1970s and 1980s like Battenberg lace collars and edgings (see page 77). These are additional items to watch for in secondhand stores and antique malls. Vintage linens and laces are fun to work with and often add inspiration to your finished pieces.

Materials list

Fabric

- 1 lace tablecloth
  or lace yardage
  sufficient to cut out
  jacket pieces

Continuous Bias

- 40 yards (36.6m)*
  ⅜" bias (pale pink)

- 40 yards (36.6m)*
  ⅜" bias (pale green)

- 8 yards (7.3m)*
  ⅝" bias (pale green)
  *NOTE: This should
  be enough for most
  sizes; however, more
  bias yardage may
  be required for sizes
  over 18 misses or for
  longer-length jackets.*

Additional Tools
& Materials

- Basic jacket pattern of
  choice

- 24"(61cm) clear
  plastic ruler with
  45°-angle marking

- Wash-away
  marking pen
  or chalk

- 1 button for
  neck closure

Heirloom Lace Jacket

Do you have one of those old lace tablecloths full of holes and stains? You can't part with it because it was your grandmother's, but you can't use it on the table anymore either.

When I first experimented with lace as a base fabric, I wondered: Would the lace be too loose and open to support the rows of chenille? Would the lace details be lost under the bias design? I needn't have worried. Chenille and lace go together perfectly.

Try using a lace tablecloth base for this Victorian-style jacket. While you're at it, make one for a mother, sister or daughter as well. She'll love sharing such a special keepsake.

instructions

1 Cut out the jacket pattern pieces from a lace tablecloth of your choice (vintage or new, or use purchased lace yardage).

2 Mark the jacket pieces with water-soluble pen. Starting at the corner, line up a 45° line on the ruler with the bottom of the piece, 2½" (6cm) from the lower corner. Continue to mark lines every 2½" (6cm) until the jacket piece is covered.

Sources of Lace

The lace you use as a fabric base does not have to come from tablecloths or new yardage. What about curtains? And the bridal department of the fabric store presents unlimited potential with all types and weights of lace to choose from.

3 Starting at the tip of the same corner, set up a 45° angle and mark lines every 2½" (6cm), with the lines slanting in the opposite direction.

Preshrinking

Shrinkage isn't a problem when using vintage tablecloths—they've been washed numerous times. However, if using new lace yardage, wash to preshrink the lace.

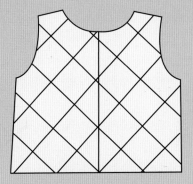
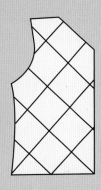
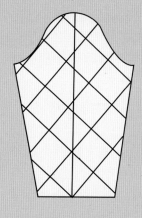

Drawing the Diamond Grid

Draw a diamond grid on all jacket pattern pieces (such as those in the example *left*). Start at the bottom center front and center back edges.

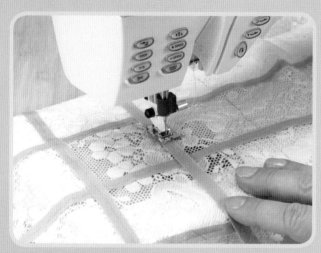

4 Using a shortened stitch length of 1.5, sew a single layer of pale green ⅜" bias on the marked diagonal lines in both directions on all jacket pieces to create the diamond grid.

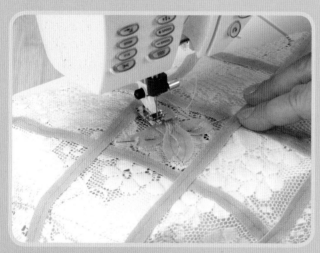

5 Cut a 9" (23cm) length of pink ⅜" bias. Sew in the center of a diamond space to make a flower, shaping as directed on page 66. Repeat for each diamond space on all jacket pieces: 2 front pieces, back and 2 sleeves.

6 Construct the jacket following pattern instructions.

7 Sew a single layer of green ⅝" bias along the raw edges on the wrong side of the jacket (around the neckline, along both front edges and the bottom and on the cuffs). Stitch the corners as instructed on page 21. The bias should extend about ⅛" (3mm) beyond the raw edges.

8 Stitch a double layer of ⅝" green bias along all the edges on the right side of the jacket, making sure the bias covers the raw edges. Sew off the corners and trim to ⅛" (3mm) beyond the cut edge.

9 Wash the finished jacket. Do not dry.

10 Tea dye the jacket (see tea-dyeing instructions on page 25). Machine dry on normal setting until the jacket is completely dry.

Lacey Leftovers Denim Vest

I found this fun Battenberg lace collar with a butterfly design in a drawer. These collars were popular on dresses in the 1980s. I think this one makes a terrific yoke detail on a denim zipper-front vest.

Watch what happens when you put a collar like this on something unexpected and embellish it with a little chenille.

For this project, use heavier sewing machine needles made especially for working with denim (or use a size 90 needle).

Materials list

Fabric

- Ready-to-wear denim vest, new or used (this project uses a zippered vest, but the vest can be any style)

- Battenberg lace collar* (purchased or reclaimed), styled to fit the back vest yoke and extend to the front of the vest
  NOTE: Battenberg lace is 100% cotton and should be preshrunk before applying to a garment.

Continuous Bias

- ⅜" bias in yellow, blue and pink to embellish lace collar (colors may vary as desired)

  - 8 yards (7.3m) ⅜" bias (pink) to accent vest front and collar

Additional Tools & Materials

- Heat-set crystals

- Heat-set applicator

1 Apply a single layer of ⅜" bias to the Battenberg lace collar using a short stitch. (Use a double layer of bias if you prefer more fullness.)

Choose and place colors appropriate to the design of your collar. (This project features a collar with a butterfly and flowers pattern embellished with blue, yellow and pink bias.)

Flip the bias wherever there's a point (leaves, etc.). See pages 50 and 52 for instructions on this procedure.

2 Sew a double layer of ⅜" bias, stitching ¼" (6mm) from the edge, down both front seams along the zipper and along the edge of the collar. (Sew additional bias along the design lines of the vest if you prefer more embellishment.)

Identifying the Right Side

Stitch bias to the right side of Battenberg lace. To identify the right side, examine both sides of the lace. Note where ends of tape within the lace have been finished, i.e., turned and stitched into place. The side of the lace with these turned ends is the *wrong* side of the lace.

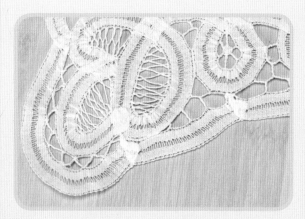

Wrong Side

Finished ends of the lace tape are marked by thicker, denser spots in the lace. These spots are visible on the *wrong* side of the lace.

To Maneuver Bias

It's helpful to have an awl or small narrow-pointed scissors to help maneuver the bias around tight corners and curves in the lace pattern.

More Tricks with Battenberg Lace

Battenberg lace edging can be embellished with chenille to create wide borders on skirts, jackets and other items.

Battenberg lace also dyes beautifully (see *below*), opening up new possibilities for using color in a project.

3 Sew the collar to the vest, following the stitching on the outer edges of the chenille.

4 Wash and dry the vest.

5 Embellish the lace with heat-set crystals as desired (see page 36 for instructions).

Luxurious Detail
This vest makes as big an impact from the back as it does from the front.

Materials list

Continuous Bias
- 40 yards (36.6m) of ⅝" bias (in color of choice)

Additional Tools & Materials
- 60" × 9½" (152cm × 24cm) piece of fabric-like water-soluble stabilizer
- Wash-away marking pen

Latticework Fringed Scarf

My first experiment stitching bias to water-soluble stabilizer was this fast and simple scarf. I added fringe and the result was the softest scarf I ever wrapped around my neck. Enjoy!

Finished size: 60" × 9½" (152cm × 24cm).

instructions

1 Cut a piece of fabric-like water-soluble stabilizer 60" × 9½" (152cm × 24cm). Mark the stabilizer with grid lines, drawing all horizontal lines first, then all vertical lines. Space lines 1¼" (32mm) apart, starting ¾" (19mm) from the edge of the stabilizer.

2 Stitch a double layer of ⅝" bias (using a 1.0 stitch length) along all the vertical lines, aligning the edge of the bias with the vertical drawn lines.

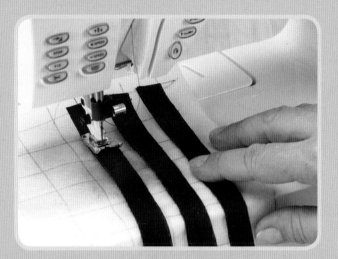

Working with Water-Soluble Stabilizer

There are wonderful stabilizers on the market today. I prefer to work on stabilizers that have a fabric-like feel and weight to them (Sulky's Fabri-Solvy™ is one I like). These stabilizers are easier to stitch, and they wash away without leaving a residue. They also hold up to marking with pens and pencils without tearing or distorting.

Test to make sure the bias sewn to the water-soluble stabilizer will have the desired effect, especially if using continuous bias cut from fabric instead of from a roll.

To make a sample: Cut an 8" (20cm) square of water-soluble stabilizer. Sew the chenille strips (using a 1.0 stitch length) to the stabilizer in a grid (see below *left*), spacing the strips the same distance apart as stated in the project instructions. Sew all the strips that go in the same direction at the same time.

Wash and dry the sample. The final result should look like the sample (see below *right*).

3 Stitch a double layer of ⅝" bias along all horizontal lines, aligning the edge of the bias with the drawn horizontal lines. Sew the horizontal bias right across the intersections with the vertical bias.

4 Prestitch a 6-yard (5.5m) length of bias and cut into twenty-four 9" (23cm) strips.

Bring the ends of 1 strip together to form a loop. Align the ends of the loop with the first strip of bias along the edge of the short end of the scarf and sew into place.

Place loops side by side along the short end of the scarf, stitching each into place in turn. Repeat at the opposite end of the scarf.

5 Rinse the scarf in the bathroom sink under cold water to wash away most of the water-soluble stabilizer. Wring out the excess water and place the scarf in the washing machine on a normal wash cycle; use a small amount of detergent to remove any remaining residue.

After washing, place the scarf in the dryer with a few old towels until completely dry.

Good Quality Thread Is a Must

Always use good quality sewing thread and a shortened stitch length when sewing on water-soluble stabilizer. If the stitching thread breaks in the washing process, you will lose the chenille and have gaping holes in your scarf.

Other Uses for Prestitched Bias Fringe

Fringe made of prestitched bias is a great embellishment for the top edge of a handbag or for the bottom or yoke of a jacket or vest.

Chenille Sweater Jacket

I couldn't believe how soft and cozy my scarves made on water-soluble stabilizer were. I wanted a jacket with that same plush feel. A chenille jacket without a fabric base layer—could it be done?

   When I wear this lightweight jacket, I'm always asked "Did you knit that yourself?" I just smile and say, "Yes, I did!"

Materials list

Fabric
- 60"-wide (152cm) fabric-like water-soluble stabilizer (yardage required for selected jacket pattern)

Continuous Bias
- 160 yards (146m)* (four 40-yard [36.5m] rolls) ⅝" continuous bias (for sizes up to 14)
NOTE: For larger sizes, use 200 yards (183m) (5 rolls).

Additional Tools & Materials
- Wash-away marking pen
- Jacket pattern of your choice
   - 6 yards (5.5m)** hand-dyed silk ribbon for weaving (optional)
   **NOTE: Yardage may vary according to the size and length of the jacket.*

instructions

1 Trace the pattern pieces onto water-soluble stabilizer. Mark the stabilizer pieces *up* to indicate the right side of the stabilizer; also mark *right side, left side, back* and *right* and *left sleeves* (according to your individual pattern) to avoid confusion when sewing on the bias strips.

2 Beginning with the right front pattern piece, align a single layer of ⅝" bias horizontally along the straight line at the bottom and stitch into place. Position and stitch additional bias strips side by side, one after another, going up the entire length of the jacket front. Extend the ends of the bias strips about ½" (13mm) beyond the pattern lines.

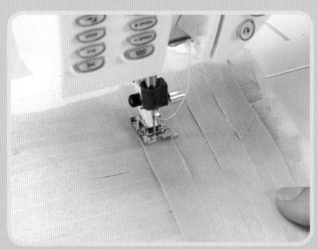

3 Redraw the center front edge line of the front pattern piece. Align the first bias strip to the center front line and stitch into place.

Align additional strips side by side and stitch into place across the front pattern piece until the piece is covered.

Repeat the entire procedure for the right front pattern piece as well as the remaining pattern pieces. Stitch the first vertical strip on the back pattern piece on the center back line and work to the sides.

4 Place the original tissue pattern piece over the bias-covered water-soluble stabilizer. Cut out the jacket piece as though cutting from actual fabric.

5 Construct the jacket according to pattern instructions. Don't finish the seams; double stitch them and trim to ¼" (6mm).

6 Make loop closures for the front of the jacket. Multiply the number of buttons you will be using for your jacket times 5" (13cm) and cut a piece of ⅝" bias that length. Example: For 3 buttons, cut a strip of bias 15" (38cm) long. Press the bias in half lengthwise, then stitch the folded bias down the middle.

Finished Seams

It's not necessary to finish seams when sewing with bias. The *blooming* of the bias conceals the seams.

7 Pin 1 end of the strip in place, form a loop large enough to accommodate the size button you're using and cut. Use this first closure strip to measure and cut the remaining closures.

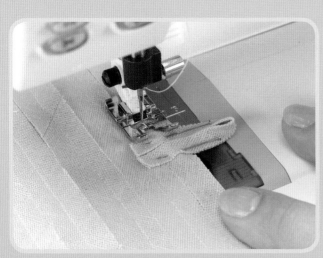

8 Pin the second end of the first closure next to the first end (both ends should be ½" [13mm] from the jacket edge). Sew down the ends of the looped bias ¼" (6mm) from the jacket edge. Repeat for the remaining closures.

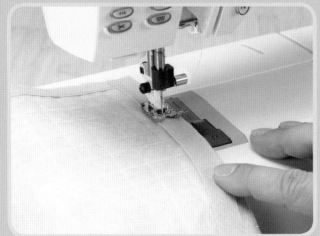

9 To finish the edges of the jacket, stitch a single layer of ⅝" bias along the underside, aligning the edge of the bias with the jacket edge. Sew all the way around the edges.

10 Sew a single layer of ⅝" bias along the edges on the right side of the jacket, including the sleeves.

11 Rinse the jacket in a sink with lukewarm water to dissolve the stabilizer, then wash on the cold water setting with ¼ cup (59ml) of cold water detergent to remove the remaining residue.

After washing, machine dry the jacket with a couple of old towels until completely dry.

12 For additional embellishment, thread ribbon through the openings in the casing along the outside edge, all the way around, starting at the neckline. Leave the ends of the ribbon long enough to tie into a bow.

Materials list

Fabric

- 60"-wide (152cm) fabric-like water-soluble stabilizer (yardage equivalent to fabric required for selected vest pattern)

Continuous Bias

- 120 yards (110m) (three 40-yard [36.6m] rolls) of ⅝" bias for vest body (pale green)

- 3"-wide (8cm) strip of fabric-like water-soluble stabilizer equivalent to the measurement of the outer edge of the vest plus 6" (15cm) for square corners or plus 10" (25cm) for front edge curves

- 25 yards (23m) ⅜" bias (natural)

- 25 yards (23m) ⅜" bias (pale green)

Additional Tools & Materials

- Vest pattern of choice (a straight-edged vest is easier, but this project uses a bolero pattern with curved edges)

- Wash-away marking pen

- 2 yards (1.8m) pearl cotton (in a natural hue) to reinforce ties

Lacey Bolero Vest

I have been designing wedding gowns for years. I love working with fine fabrics and elegant laces, and I wanted to add the look of open lacework to my chenille jackets and vests.

Simple designs and multiple colors give a new look to a textured lace edging. Instructions for making the vest begin on page 89 after a step-by-step demonstration of how to create this textured lace. The chenille lace edging takes some extra time and work, but the results are worth the effort.

demonstration

Creating Chenille Lace

1 Cut a piece of water-soluble stabilizer the desired length (see the *Materials List* on page 86) and 1½" (4cm) wider than the finished lace. Draw the design on the stabilizer starting ½" (13mm) from the edge for the first horizontal line. Draw the second horizontal line 2" (5cm) from that.

3 Stitch a single layer of ⅜" bias in color No. 1 (pale green in this example) along the top and bottom horizontal lines of the design, aligning the edges of the bias with the lines. *NOTE: Lace may be made in all 1 color of bias if desired.*

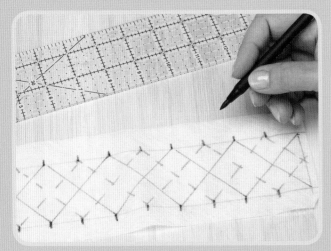

2 Make a mark every inch (25mm) along both the top and bottom horizontal lines, aligning both sets of marks. Draw a zigzag line connecting the dots, with the points of the zigzag 4" (10cm) apart. Draw a second zigzag, beginning at the mark opposite the first zigzag's starting mark, to create a diamond row.

Draw a second row of diamonds by connecting the alternating 2" (5cm) marks (between the solid lines) with dotted lines (see photo *above*).

4 Stitch the ⅜" bias in color No. 1 along the zigzag/diamond pattern drawn in solid lines. At each point, flip the bias so that it aligns with the outer edge of the border line bias. This ensures that everything that intersects is stitched; otherwise, the lace will fall apart.

5 Lay ⅜" bias in color No. 2 (natural in this example) along the zigzag/diamond pattern drawn in dotted lines, crossing the open diamond space created by color No. 1.

Repeat a second row of zigzags to complete the color No. 2 diamond pattern.

6 Trim the water-soluble stabilizer up to the upper and lower border lines.

8 Sew the prestitched bias down along 1 long side of the lace in this manner: Stitch the end of the prestitched bias into place, extending the bias ¼" (6mm) beyond the edge of the lace, and flip it. Bring the prestitched bias back down to meet the border strip of bias about 1" (25mm) from where you started, flip the bias and stitch into place.

Continue along the length of the lace, flipping the bias to make open loop points ¼" (6mm) from the edge of the border strip of bias. These loops will create a picot edge.

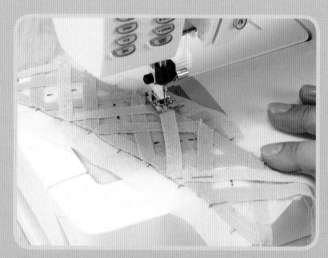

7 Prestitch a length of ⅜" bias 1½ times the length of the finished lace.

instructions

1 Trace your vest pattern of choice onto water-soluble stabilizer.

2 Mark center horizontal and vertical lines on the water-soluble stabilizer pieces. Sew ⅝" bias horizontally, then vertically, laying each bias strip next to the previous row on either side of the central line. Position the original pattern over the stabilizer pieces and trim the stabilizer to size.

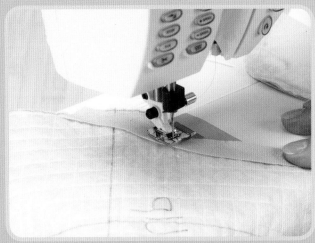

3 Sew only the shoulder seams of the vest pieces. Finish the armseye edges on the wrong side of the vest with a single layer of ⅝" bias. Begin to stitch the bias 1½" (4cm) from the side seam, sewing all the way around each armhole and ending 1½" (4 cm) from the side seam.

4 Sew the side seams of the vest. At the armholes, trim the beginning and ending segments of the bias that was sewn to the wrong side of the vest to about ½" (13mm) each, then overlap and stitch over both layers.

5 Make chenille lace according to the directions on pages 87–88.

6 Pin the lace into place ¼" (6mm) from the vest edge. If using a curved bolero pattern, make sure the bottom picot edge of the lace lies flat around the contour of the curve. Pin at the beginning and end of the curve, then make tiny pleats along the upper edge of the lace and pin. (When the chenille is washed, the fullness of the bloom will hide the pleats.)

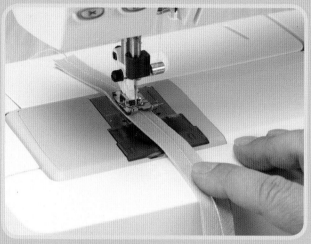

7 To make 2 ties, cut six 18" (46cm) lengths of ⅝" bias. Layer 3 strips of bias for each tie.

Center a length of pearl cotton on 1 length of layered bias. Stitching through all 3 layers of bias, sew back and forth over the end to secure the pearl cotton and all the bias layers; then couch the pearl cotton with a zigzag stitch (1.0 stitch length) down the middle of the length of bias. At the end, sew back and forth over the pearl cotton again to make sure it's secure.

Repeat for the second tie.

9 Stitch down the center of the long outside strip of bias on the lace. Be sure to catch all of the intersections of the bias to secure. (Remove each pin before stitching.)

10 Rinse the vest in a sink with lukewarm water to dissolve the stabilizer, then wash on cold water setting with ¼ cup (59ml) cold water detergent to remove remaining residue.

Put the vest in the dryer with a couple of towels until completely dry.

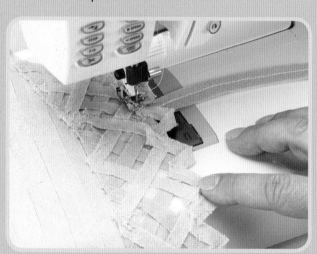

8 *Before* stitching down the lace, position the ties where desired along the front sides of the vest opening. Insert each tie between the lace and the vest edge. Sew each tie as you're stitching down the lace. Go back later and stitch the ties again along the picot stitch lines to reinforce the ties.

Embellishing Patterned Fabric

Some of the most dramatic chenille designs are created with the help of printed and patterned textiles. Take a walk through the fabric store or the linen section of a department store for instant inspiration overload.

I found that I could stitch continuous bias to almost anything, whether it was a beach towel or just an interesting piece of home decorator fabric that had a dramatic design. Here are a few suggestions as you look for unexpected finds.

Stitching Bias to Bold Florals

A textile with a bold floral design can be transformed into a colorful, textured fabric with a whole new look.

Lay continuous bias following the lines and contours of the pattern (left), taking color cues from the design itself or choosing complimentary colors for a contrasting effect.

Ordinary Fabric Transformed

The completed sample (left) shows the richness that chenille details can add to an ordinary piece of fabric.

Don't be afraid to experiment with different design details and degrees of embellishment to explore the possibilities of your base fabric.

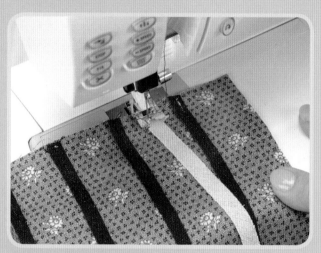

Unexpected Design Lines Within Textile Patterns

Use your imagination when looking at a fabric for inspiration, and keep your eyes open for unexpected design lines within a pattern.

The layout of the flowers on this dotted material (above) provides ready-made design lines for stitching continuous bias into place.

Creating Stripes and Plaids

Alternating single strips of burgundy and cream bias result in a striped texture (above *left*).

Crossing those strips with single lines of alternating burgundy and cream bias (still following the flower pattern) produces a plaid (above *right*).

Following Diagonal Lines

Laying bias along diagonal lines on a patterned fabric (above) is another way to explore new possibilities for texture and color.

Design lines do not have to be solid to provide a good guide for stitching down straight lines of bias.

Experiment for Different Results

Experiment by creating various samples with bias stitched along different design lines; then study the variety of effects you achieve.

Consider whether you want more or fewer lines of chenille, how much of the fabric's design you want to show in the background, as well as the effect of different colors of bias against your base fabric.

Plaid Chenille Tote

I used a simple print fabric as the base to create the plaid chenille fabric for this tote. Being able to follow the rows of print on the fabric makes it easy to lay down the rows of bias without any marking.

Finishing the edges and straps with bias strips makes this project fast to complete. It also eliminates bulky seams and embellishes at the same time.

Finished size: 13" × 15½" (33cm × 39cm).

Materials list

Fabric

- ¾ yard (69cm) chenille-embellished plaid fabric*
  *NOTE: The fabric pattern should contain good lines for laying down the plaid chenille design; see Embellishing Patterned Fabric (pages 91-92) for technique details.
- ¾ yard (69cm) fusible fleece
- 1¼ yards (1.1m) 45"-wide (114cm) coordinating fabric (for lining and pockets)
- Piece of floral-patterned fabric (for creating appliqué)

Continuous Bias

- 6 yards (5.5m) ⅝" bias (color[s] to coordinate with bag fabric)

Additional Tools & Materials

- Piece of fusible web to fit appliqué
- Coordinating machine embroidery threads

instructions

1 Create chenille-embellished fabric as directed in the demonstration on pages 91-92. Cut two 15" × 18" (38cm × 46cm) pieces from the embellished fabric.

2 Cut 2 pieces of fusible fleece the same size as the chenille-embellished fabric pieces. Iron to fuse the fleece to each fabric piece (follow the manufacturer's instructions).

3 Cut a piece of the floral-patterned fabric containing a large floral motif to use as an appliqué for the front of the bag. Iron fusible web to the back of the floral fabric piece.

4 Cut out the appliqué motif, trimming right up to the motif outline.

5 Peel off the paper backing and iron the appliqué to fuse it into position on the chenille-embellished fabric piece that will serve as the bag's front.

6 Stitch around the outline of the flower, just inside the edge; then stitch around the leaves. Thread-paint details over the design (see page 34 for a more detailed discussion of this process).

7 Put the 2 bag pieces together, right sides facing, and stitch the sides with a ¼" (6mm) seam allowance. Sew across the bottom of the bag, also with a ¼" (6mm) seam allowance.

8 At 1 corner of the bag, press the side and bottom seams together and open both seams. Pin to keep the corner flat and the seams open.
  Measure 2½" (6cm) down from the point this creates and draw a line across the corner. Stitch over this line. Trim the seam to ¼"(6mm).
  Repeat this procedure on the opposite corner.

9 Zigzag stitch around the top edge of the bag. Turn the bag.

10 Cut two 2½" × 31" (6cm × 79cm) pieces of the original unembellished bag fabric. Cut 2 pieces of fusible fleece the same width and length as the bag fabric strips. Fuse together 1 fabric strip and 1 fleece strip for each strap.

No Turn Technique

Turning each edge of the strap to the middle provides finished edges without having to sew and turn the entire strap. The bias sewn down the center of the strap further finishes the strap.

11 With the right side of 1 strap facing down, draw a line lengthwise down the center of that strap (1¼" [3cm] from the edge) on the fleece side.

Bring 1 raw edge of the strap to the center and sew into place using a zigzag stitch (4.0 stitch length).

Repeat for the second raw edge of the strap.

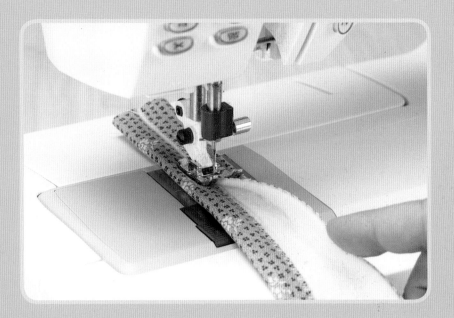

12 Sew a double layer of ⅝" bias down the center of each strap to cover the raw edges. (Be sure to sew to the side of the strap with the stitched-down raw edges. This will be the *right* side of the strap when finished.)

13 Position the end of each strap 4½" (11cm) from each side seam along the top edge of the bag on both long sides. With the right side up, insert the end of the strap ½" (13mm) into the bag and stitch ¼" (6mm) from the top edge of bag.

Repeat for the remaining strap ends.

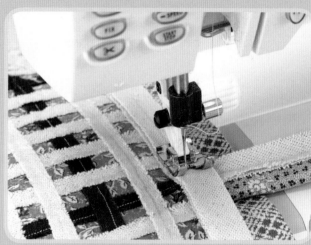

14 For the lining, cut two 18" × 19" (46cm × 48cm) pieces from a coordinating cotton print. Assemble the lining as you did the bag, sewing the sides first, then the bottom, leaving a ¼" (6mm) seam allowance. Match the seams at the corners, mark lines, then stitch and trim (see Step 8).

16 Sew a double layer of ⅝" bias around the edge of the bag (the edge of the bias should extend about ⅛" [3mm] beyond the edge of bag), overlapping the ends where they meet.

15 Insert the lining into the bag, wrong sides together, leaving ¾" (19mm) of the lining above the top edge of the bag. Press 3" (8cm) from the top edge into the bag. Pin the lining into place.

Stitch along the top outside edge of the bag all the way around.

17 Wash and dry the bag.

Altered Towel Beach Bag

What could be more fun than this terry cloth beach bag heavily embellished with chenille? Today's towel designs will inspire new ways to create chenille patterns for the perfect bag (and possibly a matching cover-up).

NOTE: Your towel and washcloth can be any size; this project was designed with a 19" × 30" (48cm × 76cm) hand towel and a 13" x 13½" (33cm × 34cm) washcloth. Choose colors and patterns that appeal to you.

Materials list

Fabric

- 1 large terry cloth hand towel, approximately 19" × 30" (48cm × 76cm)

- 1 terry cloth washcloth, approximately 13" x 13½" (33cm × 34cm)

Continuous Bias

- 25 yards (23m) ⅜" bias (color[s] to match your towel design)

- 25 yards (23m) ⅝" bias (color[s] to match your towel design)

- 3 yards (2.7m) prepleated ⅝" bias (white)

Additional Tools & Materials

- Assorted buttons for embellishment

97

instructions

1 Layer a single strip of ⅜" bias on top of a single strip of ⅝" bias. Sew the layered bias strips to the towel as desired to embellish (use the pattern of your towel as inspiration).

3 Pin the pocket to the towel, centering 1½" (4cm) from each side and aligning the raw edge of the trimmed washcloth with the finished bottom of the towel.

Sew down both sides of the pocket. Sew along the bottom with a zigzag stitch (where the edge meets the towel).

2 Trim the washcloth to 10" (25cm) deep along 1 side only; the finished sides are left as is.

Embellish the washcloth with pleated ⅝" bias in a pattern of your choice. (Simple stripes or latticework designs work well.)

Embellish with fun buttons as desired.

Tips for Working With Terry Cloth

When embellishing a highly textured fabric such as terry cloth, it's necessary to use double layers of bias to create enough heft and fluff. Sewing on terry cloth is like sewing on velvet—it moves around. Use extra pressure to press down the nap of the terry cloth while stitching the bias.

If you have a walking foot for your machine, you'll find it helpful when stitching terry cloth, and it will keep the bias from slipping.

6 Make a cord as instructed on page 90 (follow the instructions for making ties in Step 7), using 4 layers of bias instead of 3, and 3–4 strands of pearl cotton.

Wash the cord separately from the beach bag. When dry, insert the cord through the bag casing and tie in a bow.

4 Turn the top edge down 2" (5cm) for the casing. Stitch into place along the finish line.

5 Bring the 2 edges of the towel together and sew along the side and across the bottom to complete the bag.

A Matching Cover-Up

Make a bathing suit cover-up, using a sewing pattern of your choice, from a towel and washcloths that match your beach bag (see page 101 of the gallery at the end of this chapter).

Gallery

I added interest to this scarf by changing the shape slightly so that it rolls back for a shawl collar effect. This scarf has also been hand-painted with textile pens (after it was washed but before it was dried). The hand painting gives the chenille flecks of color; the inks are heat-set when the scarf goes into the dryer.

Decorator fabric provides the base and the floral appliqué for this elegant travel bag. Multiple colors and widths of bias create texture on the plaid fabric while thread-painting adds dimension to the appliqué. The centers of the flowers are embellished with heat-set crystals for a finishing touch.

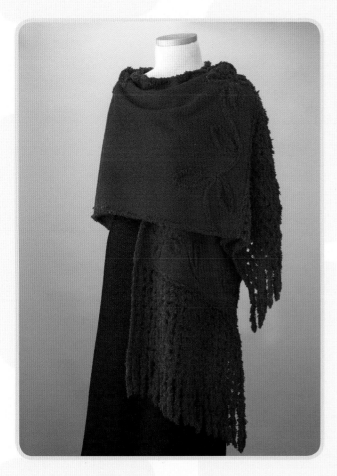

Touches of chenille give this comfortable plush polar fleece wrap an elegant flair.

Prepleated ⅝" bias was used for the red-on-red flower and winding design on the front and back edges. A latticework panel was stitched on water-soluble stabilizer and attached to the bottom of the front and back panels.

A fringe of prestitched ⅝" bias at the base of the latticework adds a final touch.

Use the commercial sewing pattern of your choice and full-size bath towels to create a matching cover-up for your chenille-trimmed *Altered Towel Beach Bag* (page 97). Colors and patterns available in today's towels provide an incredible array of design possibilities for stitching with chenille. Look for a cover-up sewing pattern with minimal seams; use the finished seams of the towels wherever possible to eliminate edges that require additional finishing.

Chapter Five

Chenille Texture at Home

Many of us remember vintage bedspreads with row after row of chenille tufts or have seen them at antique shows and malls. With such a tradition of chenille in the home, it's only natural to find new ways to add that vintage look and feel to home decorating projects.

See how appealing blankets and comforters become adorned with soft raised designs. Children love a favorite blanket that is cuddly and colorful.

Using continuous bias as text on quilts and wall hangings or to accent designs gives these pieces dimension. The possibilities seem to be endless when it comes to adding chenille accents at home. Here are a few of my favorites.

Materials list

Fabric

- 11" × 31" (28cm × 79cm) cream cotton Fabric A (background)
- ⅛ yard (11cm) print Fabric B (first graduated border)
- ¼ yard (23cm) print Fabric C (second graduated border)
- ¼ yard (23cm) print Fabric B or C (quilt sleeve)
- ⅜ yard (34cm) black cotton Fabric D (third graduated border)
- ¼ yard (23cm) black cotton Fabric D (binding)
- 18" × 37" (46cm × 94cm) print Fabric E (backing)

Continuous Bias

- 7 yards (6.4m) ⅜" bias (wine)

Additional Tools & Materials

- 18" × 37" (46cm × 94cm) cotton batting

Home Sweet Home
Wall Hanging

Chenille provides a fast and easy way to say something special on a small wall quilt for your home. Make it look handwritten or copy your favorite font onto paper for a pattern.

I liked this home-style look for a traditional sentiment in our family room.

Finished size: 19½" x 38" (50cm × 97cm).

instructions

1 Cut an 11" × 31" (28cm × 79cm) panel from Fabric A. Enlarge and photocopy *Home Sweet Home* from the template on page 125 (or create your own). Transfer the text to the panel, positioning as indicated in the photo.

2 Sew each letter with a double layer of ⅜" bias using a 1.5 stitch length. Stitch down the middle of the bias following the lines of each letter.

3 From Fabric B, cut two ¾" × 13½" (19mm × 34cm) and two ¾" × 31½" (19mm × 80cm) strips for the first set of graduated borders. With right sides together, attach 1 long strip to 1 side of the background panel using a ¼" (6mm) seam. Press the band to the side.

Repeat on the opposite side, then attach the short strips to the 2 panel ends. Trim at the corners so the edges are straight and squared.

4 From Fabric C, cut two 1¾" × 15½" (4cm × 39cm) and two 1¾" × 34" (4cm × 86cm) strips. Attach to the first border following the instructions in Step 3. Trim the corners.

5 From Fabric D, cut two 3" × 20" (8cm × 51cm) and two 3" × 38" (8cm × 97cm) strips. Attach to the second border following instructions in Step 3. Trim the corners.

6 Layer the finished top with batting and backing (Fabric E). Quilt the wall hanging as desired; bind using Fabric D. If desired, create a tube from Fabric B or C and attach along the upper back edge as a sleeve to hold a dowel or rod for hanging.

Materials list

Fabric

- ¾ yard (69cm) 42–45"-wide (107–114cm) Fabric A (dark green pattern)

- ¾ yard (69cm) 42–45"-wide Fabric B (golden plaid)

- ¾ yard (69cm) 42–45"-wide Fabric C (golden floral)

- ⅝ yard (57cm) 42–45"-wide Fabric D (large floral with enough flowers for 30 large motifs)

- 2 yards (1.8m) 42–45"-wide Fabric E (backing, can be pieced from leftover fabric)

Continuous Bias

- 65 yards (59.4m) ⅜" bias (in a complimentary color)

- 14 yards (12.8m) ⅝" bias (in a complimentary color)

Additional Tools & Materials

- 52" × 60" (132cm × 152cm) cotton batting (low loft or needle punched)

Simple Pieced Throw

A simple pieced quilt is simplified even more by using chenille to embellish and quilt in one easy step. I've also found I can eliminate the traditional bound edge (and the work it involves) by finishing my quilts with a soft, plush edge of chenille.

Be sure to wash the fabric to preshrink it before cutting out the blocks.

Finished size: 54" × 64" (1.4m × 1.6m)—11 blocks × 13 rows.

instructions

1 Cut the fabric into 5" (13cm) blocks as follows:
   Fabric A (42 blocks)
   Fabric B (35 blocks)
   Fabric C (36 blocks)
   Fabric D (30 blocks).
   You should have a total of 143 blocks (the throw is 11 blocks by 13 blocks).

2 Using a ¼" (6mm) seam allowance, piece the blocks into 2 separate rows.
   Row 1: Fabric A / B / A / B / A / B / A / B / A / B / A.
   Row 2: Fabric C / D / C / D / C / D / C / D / C / D / C.
   Press the seams in opposite directions.

3 Sew the rows together, alternating Row 1 and Row 2. Press the seams in opposite directions. When assembled, the throw should begin and end with Row 1.

4 Cut low-loft batting (or needle-punched cotton batting) and backing material 1" (25mm) bigger than the quilt top all the way around. The backing can be pieced from leftover fabric.

5 Layer the quilt top, batting and backing. Pin at the center of each block.

Layout of the Throw
The diagram (right) shows the piecing sequence for Rows 1 and 2 and the order for attaching the rows to assemble the throw.

Nine Patch as Pillow

Blocks can be assembled as a Nine Patch (*below*) to make a matching pillow top.

A	B	A	B	A	B	A	B	A	B	A
C	D	C	D	C	D	C	D	C	D	C
A	B	A	B	A	B	A	B	A	B	A
C	D	C	D	C	D	C	D	C	D	C
A	B	A	B	A	B	A	B	A	B	A
C	D	C	D	C	D	C	D	C	D	C
A	B	A	B	A	B	A	B	A	B	A
C	D	C	D	C	D	C	D	C	D	C
A	B	A	B	A	B	A	B	A	B	A
C	D	C	D	C	D	C	D	C	D	C
A	B	A	B	A	B	A	B	A	B	A
C	D	C	D	C	D	C	D	C	D	C
A	B	A	B	A	B	A	B	A	B	A

6 Lay down a double layer of ³⁄₈" bias over the crosswise seams and stitch into place with a 2.0 stitch length. Repeat on the vertical rows. *NOTE: This process embellishes and quilts the throw in one step.*

8 Finish the throw with a double layer of ⁵⁄₈" bias on the top and bottom sides. (See page 21 for additional tips on finishing edges with chenille.)

9 Machine wash and dry the throw.

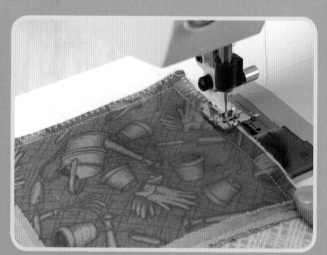

7 Trim the excess batting and backing from the edges. Stitch ¼" (6mm) from the edge of the quilt all the way around, then zigzag stitch directly over the raw edges.

Like Stained Glass

Outlining kaleidoscope designs with ³⁄₈" black bias will give your quilts a stained glass look.

Strip-Pieced Baby Blanket

One of the first techniques you learn as a new quilter is how to strip-piece a quilt. I've used this quilting basic to create a fast way to make colorful chenille blocks for the ultimate baby blanket.

There's an advantage to using waffle cloth for this project: It's easy to follow the lines in the cloth when sewing the bias.

Finished size: 36" × 40" (91cm × 102cm)—9 blocks × 10 rows.

Materials list

Fabric
- 1 yard (1m)
  60"-wide (152cm)
  or
  1¼ yards (1.1m)
  45"-wide (114cm)
  cotton waffle cloth
- 1¼ yards (1.1m)
  60"-wide (152cm)
  or
  1½ yards (1.4m)
  45"-wide (114cm)
  coordinating fabric
  (backing)

Continuous Bias
- 25 yards (23m)
  ⅜" bias for strips
  (pale pink)
- 25 yards (23m)
  ⅜" bias for strips
  (pale yellow)
- 12½ yards (11.4m)
  ⅜" bias for strips
  (pale green)
- 17 yards (15.5m)
  ⅝" bias for
  binding
  (pale pink)

Additional Tools & Materials
- 6" (15cm) ruler
- 38" × 42"
  (97cm × 107cm)
  cotton batting

instructions

1 Cut 4¼"-wide (11cm) strips from the full width of the waffle cloth.

2 Fold a waffle cloth strip in half lengthwise and press. Unfold.

3 Starting at the center, using the fold as a guide, stitch a single layer of ⅜" bias down the center of the strip using a 1.5 stitch length. Continue to sew 4 more strips, 2 on either side of the center bias strip, for a total of 5 strips ⅜" (10mm) apart. Repeat for each of the remaining waffle cloth strips.

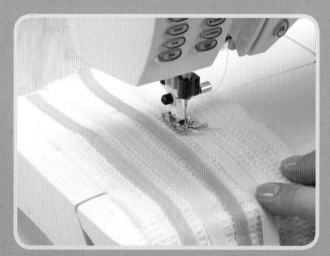

4 Cut the bias-striped waffle cloth strips every 4½"(11cm) to create blocks. (Three strips can be stacked and cut at one time.) A 6"(15cm) ruler works especially well for this step.

5 Piece the blocks with the bias stripes running in alternate directions. Use a ¼" (6mm) seam allowance. Press the seams in opposite directions.

6 Cut the backing and batting 1" (25mm) bigger all around than the finished quilt size. Layer the backing, batting and quilt top. Pin the center of each square.

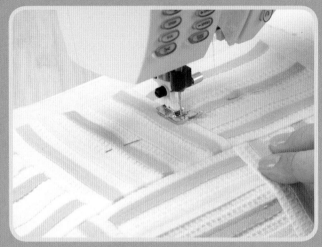 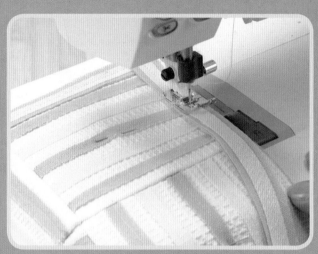

7 To quilt, stitch in the ditch, sewing just inside the seam lines on each block. Sew all the seams that go in one direction, then sew all seams that go in the other direction.

9 Stitch a double layer of ⅝" bias along the top and bottom edges of the blanket all the way around, extending the edge of the bias ⅛" (3mm) beyond the blanket edge. (If desired, you can layer a ⅜" strip of yellow bias over the double layer of ⅝" pink bias for added dimension.)

8 Trim the excess batting and backing from the edges of the blanket. Stitch ¼" (6mm) from the edge of the blanket all the way around, then zigzag stitch directly over the raw edges of the blanket.

10 Machine wash and dry the blanket.

Layering Different Widths

Layering a ⅜" bias strip in a contrasting color over ⅝" bias on the finished edge of a quilt top is a good way to add dimension and detail.

Materials list

Fabrics

- Light blue patterned fabrics (or colors as desired)*
- Dark blue patterned fabrics (or colors as desired)*
  *NOTE: Leftovers or fat quarters, enough for sixteen 4" (10cm) squares and 2 contrasting flower appliqués.
- 2 yards (1.8m) loosely woven cotton (pretested) for 2"-wide (5cm) bias

Continuous Bias

- 3 yards (2.7m) ⅜" bias (white)
- 2 yards (1.8m) ⅜" bias (pale green)

Additional Tools & Materials

- 2 yards (1.8m) ¼" (6mm) cotton cord
- 2 yards (1.8m) jumbo rickrack (green)
- ⅜ yard (0.3m) 17"-wide (43cm) paper-backed fusible web
- 16" (41cm) pillow form
- Piping foot or zipper foot

Flower Appliqué Pillow

Adding bias accents and embellishment (like the jumbo rickrack on this pillow) to appliqué designs makes them pop, whether the project is a pillow top or quilt.

I have always used piping as a way to give seams a finished look. The new piping technique in this project gives a soft chenille edging to the reversed piping finish.

Finished size: 16" × 16" (41cm × 41cm).

instructions

1 Cut sixteen 4" (10cm) squares from light and dark blue printed fabrics.

2 Using a ¼" (6mm) seam allowance, piece 4 blocks per row, positioning colors and prints as desired. Press seams to 1 side.

3 Photocopy the flower templates on page 115, enlarging as indicated. Trace the pattern onto fusible web, starting with the circle of even-numbered petals first. Make a separate tracing of the circle of odd-numbered petals.

4 Select a separate fabric for each flower, chosen to contrast well with the light and dark patterned fabrics in the pieced background. Iron to fuse each circle of flower petals to its respective fabric. Do not peel off the paper backing.

5 Trace the center circles of the flowers onto fusible web. Set aside.

6 Starting with 1 flower, cut out each petal separately. Use the numbers on the paper backing of the fusible web as a guide to position the petals counterclockwise in reverse numerical order. Once all of the petals are in position, peel off the paper backing and press to fuse each petal into place.

Repeat this process for the second flower.

7 Cut 2 stems from green jumbo rickrack. Each stem should be long enough to reach from the flower head to the bottom of the pillow top. Stitch into place, sewing down the center of the rickrack.

8 Cut one 5" (13cm) piece of green jumbo rickrack for the small flower leaves and one 8" (20cm) piece for the large flower leaves. Shape each rickrack strip into a V and position the point over the rickrack stem. Stitch leaves into place down the middle of both arms of the rickrack V.

9 Stitch a single layer of ⅜" bias (using a 1.5 stitch length) down the center of the stem rickrack. Next, stitch ⅜" bias down the center of each leg of the V-shaped leaf.

10 Cut out the flower center circles and iron to fuse to the middle of the petal circles on the pillow top.

11 Sew a continuous single layer of ⅜" bias along the edge of each flower petal, flipping the bias at each base and point. Once the petals are sewn, stitch ⅜" bias round the center circle on each flower.

12 Assemble the front and back of the pillow following the directions for the *Vintage Pillow* on page 65. Bind the edges with a simple ⅜" (10mm) binding.

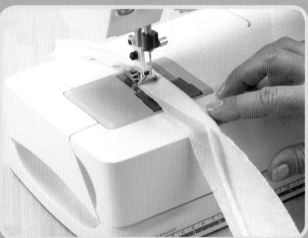

13 Cut a 1½" x 35" (4cm x 89cm) strip of bias from pretested loosely woven cotton. (See pages 18–19 for information about testing fabric for use as continuous bias.) Cut a 37" (94cm) length of ¼" (6mm) cotton cord.

Fold the bias strip in half lengthwise, placing the cotton cord within the fold. Using a zipper foot, stitch the folded bias as close as possible to the cord.

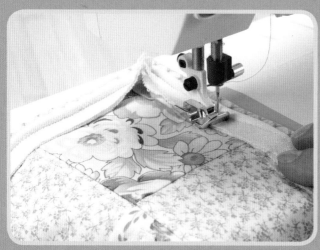

14 Use the zipper foot to sew the cording along the edge of the pillow's binding, stitching into the binding seam. At the corner, clip the raw edge of the cording to the cording seam. Position the cording to round the corner neatly, keeping the raw cut edges free.

Continue to sew each side of the pillow top, finishing the corners as described above.

15 Machine wash and dry the pillow cover. Insert the pillow form through the back flap.

Flower Appliqué Templates
Template A (above) goes at the top of the pillow. Template B (left) goes at the bottom. Enlarge both by 50%.

Materials list

Fabric

- 1 yard (1m) Fabric A (background, center heart patch)
- ⅝ yard (0.6m) Fabric B (heart patches, on-point diamond, borders, binding)
- ¼ yard (0.2m) Fabric C (heart patches)
- 1 yard (1m) backing fabric

Continuous Bias

- 4 yards (3.7m) ⅜" bias (dark brown) for heart edging and grid lines
- 3 yards (2.7m) ⅝" prepleated bias (dark brown) for outer edge of wall hanging

Additional Tools & Materials

- Old photos to scan
- Photo transfer fabric
- Paper for making heart template
- 1¼ yards (1.2m) lace trim (horizontal grid lines on heart)
- ½ yard (.5m) 1¼"-wide (32mm) lace (heart-shaped edging)
- Mementos and keepsakes for embellishments

Keepsake Wall Hanging

Because chenille brings back so many memories, I wanted that texture in this nostalgic wall hanging, which showcases some precious mementos I had tucked away in drawers and special boxes.

Get out your old photos and go on a treasure hunt for keepsakes that will give this piece an extra personal touch.

Finished size: 27" × 29.5" (69cm × 75cm). (See page 117 for tips on how to adjust the size of this project.)

instructions

1 Select photos you'd like to reproduce for the wall hanging and scan them. (If you don't have a scanner, take them to a copy store or have the photo center of your local retailer scan your photos to a disk.)

Use your computer to size the scanned images to fit the dimensions of the heart pattern pieces for the wall hanging. Print the photos onto pretreated fabric made especially for photo transfers (available at most craft stores; follow manufacturer's instructions).

2 Create a heart template (see directions below *right*). Divide the heart into thirds in both directions and mark, creating 9 individual blocks. Number the blocks from left to right, top to bottom, to make it easier to reassemble the heart. Cut the heart template into the 9 blocks.

3 Choose which fabric you want to use for each heart piece. (Use the photo on page 116 as a guide or make up your own layout pattern.)

Using the individual templates, cut out the heart pieces, adding a ¼" (6mm) seam allowance to the inner edges. *Do not* add a seam allowance to the outer edges of the heart pieces.

4 Position the photo transfers as desired on the appropriate heart patches. Fabric edges can be left raw. Sew the transfers in place using pearl cotton and a blanket stitch (can be machine-sewn or hand-embroidered).

5 Cut a 4½" (11cm) block from Fabric C. Stitch on-point to the center heart patch using a blanket stitch. The edges of the block may be left raw.

Adjusting the Size

You can adjust the size of the hanging easily. To make your hanging smaller or larger, cut your background fabric to the dimensions you wish—include ¼" (6mm) all around for the seam allowance. Cut a square of paper the size of the heart that will go on your hanging (be sure to leave adequate room for the background around the heart) and follow the directions on this page (right) for completing your template. Sew and finish your hanging as instructed.

Creating a Heart Template

Take a piece of paper about the size of the heart you want for your hanging and fold the paper in half. Draw half of the heart design along the fold in the paper and cut it out. When opened, you'll have a heart with evenly matched sides that's in proportion to the size of your wall hanging.

6 Form a heart shape from lace trim and stitch it to the on-point square in the center heart patch.

7 Stitch the 9 heart blocks together. Re-assemble the numbered heart template pieces to use as a guide.)

9 With a zigzag stitch, sew lace to the 2 horizontal seams on the heart, centering the lace on the seams. Next, sew a single layer of ⅜" bias down the center of the lace, making sure you don't completely cover it. Sew a single layer of ⅜" bias to the outer edge of the heart as well as to the vertical seams.

10 Cut four 1½" × 30" (4cm × 76cm) borders from Fabric B. Sew the borders to the edges of the center panel (it's not necessary to miter the corners).

11 Layer the completed wall hanging, batting and backing. Bind and quilt the wall hanging as desired (see page 107–108 for additional helpful information).

8 Cut a 25" × 27" (64cm × 69cm) panel from Fabric A. Center the pieced heart on the background panel and pin into place. Zigzag stitch around the edges of the heart with a 3.5 stitch.

12 Sew ⅝" prepleated bias along the seam line of the border. (See page 22 for instructions on creating prepleated bias.)

Cutting the Heart Patches

Divide your heart pattern according to this diagram, cutting your fabric as indicated.

13 Arrange your memorabilia and any additional embellishments on the quilt top. Sew the memorabilia and embellishments into place.

Personalized Embellishments

My wall hanging is a tribute to my great-grandmother and includes her photographs as well as small mementos including her reading glasses, pieces of jewelry, old buttons from some of her dresses and even an old key from one of her trunks.

A wall hanging like this is also great for baby mementos or personal achievement awards. Gloves, handkerchiefs, political buttons—there are endless possibilities for turning memorabilia into personalized embellishments.

Gallery

(Left) This picture of my precious grandchildren, printed onto fabric, stands out on this pillow thanks to rows of ⅝" bias, which create a textured frame.

Using double layers of bias to finish the edges of the pillow eliminates the bulk of the heavy decorator fabric—I didn't have to turn and finish any edges, and I could be sure that my corners were perfect.

(Below) Create a wall hanging for a child's room using simple designs from a coloring book or favorite storybook. Cut the shapes out of fabric, such as this train, and appliqué to the background.

Children's photos printed onto pretreated cotton fabric give a personalized touch to the train cars, which I sewed with decorative stitching before placing the train cars on the background.

The final touch was accenting the cars and wheels with ⅜" bias to give the wall hanging dimension and texture. The clouds and the smoke from the engine are prepleated ⅝" bias.

With the strip quilting technique explained on pages 109–111, you can use your choice of fabrics and colors to make throws or even full-size quilts. I used two coordinating small print quilting cottons for this family room throw. The strips were stitched with single layers of natural and navy ⅜" bias, then cut and laid out in an alternating design. Stitch-in-the-ditch quilting and edges finished with ⅝" bias make it possible to complete a quilt like this over a weekend.

Home decorator fabrics can become fashion apparel as well, as in the case of this jacket, which uses a vintage throw as a base. Use your favorite jacket pattern as the perfect canvas for this simple traditional chenille design, which is simply repeated over the surface of the jacket. The sleeve pattern is stitched in ⅜" continuous bias; ⅜" bias also outlines the flower detailing on the shoulders. Finishing the edges with ⅝" bias eliminates the need for facing and hems. It also reduces bulk, saves time and ties everything together—keeping the edges soft while completing the chenille design.

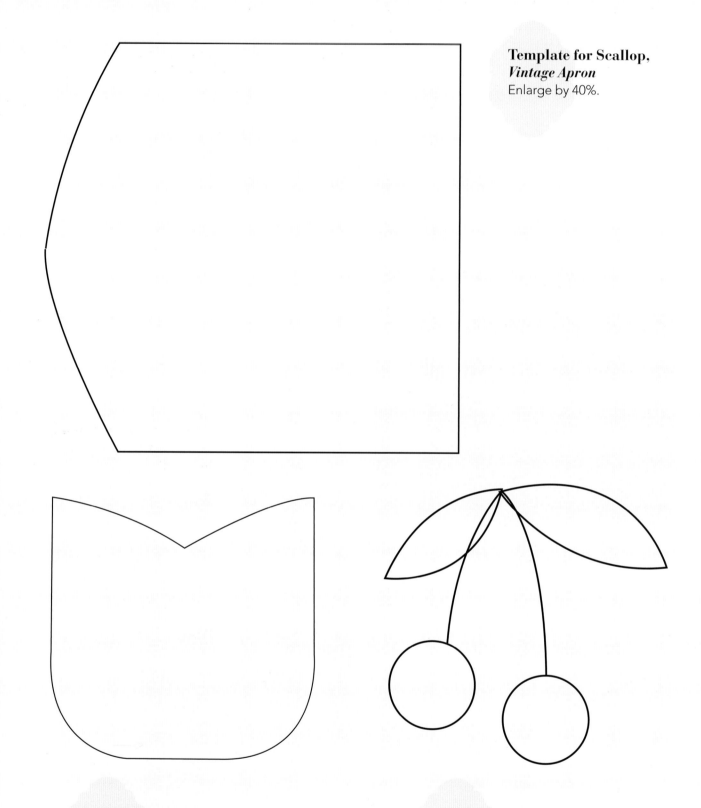

Template for Scallop,
Vintage Apron
Enlarge by 40%.

Template for Pocket,
Vintage Apron
Enlarge by 60%.

Template for Cherry Design,
Vintage Apron Pot Holder
Enlarge by 30%.

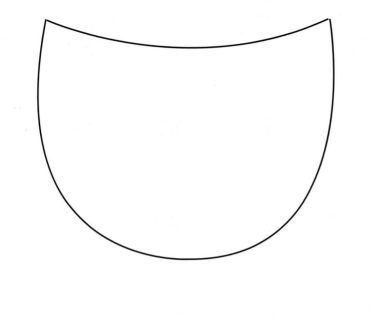

Template for Pocket,
Sunflower Apron
Enlarge by 40%.

Template for Sunflower Head,
Sunflower Apron
Enlarge by 60%.

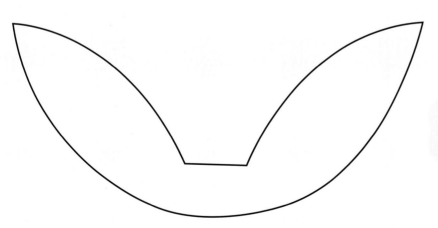

Template for Leaf Appliqué,
Sunflower Apron
Enlarge by 40%.

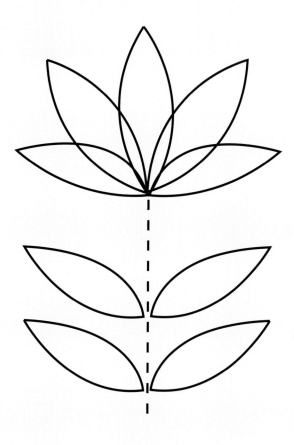

Template for
Ring of Flowers Skirt
Enlarge by 15%.

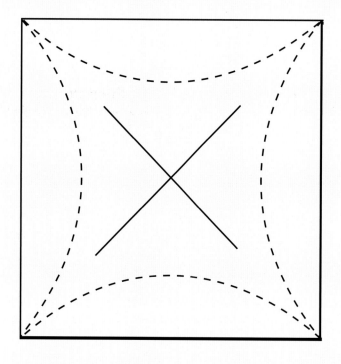

Chenille Pattern for *Vintage Pillow* **and** *Vintage-Style Jacket*
Enlarge by 40%.

Template for *Home* in
Home Sweet Home Wall Hanging
Enlarge by 50%.
Use pattern twice.

Template for *Sweet* in
Home Sweet Home Wall Hanging
Enlarge by 60%.

Resources

Chenille-It™ Blooming Bias™
www.fauxchenille.com
(801) 485-6806
(Chenille-It™ Blooming Bias™ continuous bias
and patterns, traditional chenille patterns)

Things Japanese
www.silkthings.com
(425) 821-2287
(heat-set dyes, ready-to-dye bias silk ribbon)

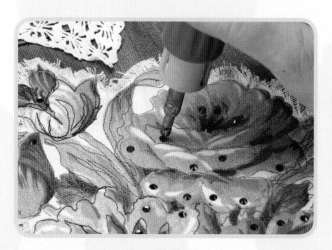

Kandi Corp
www.kandicorp.com
(800) 985-2634
(heat-set applicators, crystals, studs
and embellishments)

Sulky of America
www.sulky.com
(800) 874-4115
(embroidery threads, stabilizers)

**Look for these products in craft stores and
quilt and fabric shops, or check online.**

Index

Add More Fiber to Your Life

Claire Shaeffer's Fabric Sewing Guide, 2nd Edition
Claire Shaeffer

This full-color edition of the ultimate one-stop sewing resource is great for new and savvy sewers alike, with easy-to-read charts for needle sizes and thread and stabilizer types. Paperback, 528 pages, #Z0933.

ISBN 13: 978-0-89689-536-2

ISBN-10: 0-89689-536-X

Felting
The Complete Guide
Jane Davis

Discover felting in all its different forms: fiber, needle and knitted and crocheted felting, each in its own section. Includes 35+ projects and inspirational ideas. Hardcover with concealed wire binding, 256 pages, #Z1479.

ISBN 13: 978-0-89689-590-4

ISBN-10: 0-89689-590-4.

Strands
Creating Unexpected Fabrics and Fashionable Projects
Jacqueline Myers-Cho

Learn to handcraft original fabric designs using repurposed or simple materials such as thread, tape, plastic bags, paper and more. Then discover how to use these innovative creations to craft fashion-forward projects like purses, scarves and hats. Paperback, 128 pages, #Z2319.

ISBN 13: 978-1-60061-137-7

ISBN-10: 1-60061-137-0

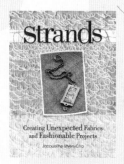

The Art of Manipulating Fabric
Colette Wolff

Presenting an encyclopedia of techniques to resurface, reshape, restructure and reconstruct fabric. More than 350 diagrams show how to begin with the simplest flat piece of cloth and progress to a beautiful finished tapestry. Paperback, 320 pages, #AOMF.

ISBN 13: 978-0-8019-8496-9

ISBN-10: 0-8019-8496-3

Thread Painting
Simple Techniques to Add Texture and Dimension
Leni Levenson Wiener

Use your sewing machine, computer and creativity to design stunning custom fabric art through thread painting. Identify various threads, tension and bobbins to use, while you create 15+ projects including totes, pillows and artwork for your home. Paperback, 128 pages, #Z0379.

ISBN-13: 978-0-89689-435-8

ISBN-10: 0-89689-435-5